ART & PHILOSOPHY

Timothy Taubes

 **Prometheus Books**

59 John Glenn Drive
Buffalo, New York 14228-2197

For Frank, Laura, Chung, and Frederic

Published 1993 by Prometheus Books

97 96 95 94 93   5 4 3 2 1

Library of Congress Cataloging-in-Publication Data

Taubes, Timothy.
    Art and philosophy / Timothy Taubes.
        p.   cm.
    Includes bibliographical references.
    ISBN 0-87975-865-1
    1. Art—Philosophy. 2. Aesthetics, Modern—20th century. I. Title.
BH39.T395   1993
111'.85—dc20   93-36085
                                                                CIP

Printed in the United States of America on acid-free paper.

Contents

Part One

PHILOSOPHY

Preface

Part One outlines a certain way of looking at art, but not the only way. It proceeds from the standpoint that art is an occurrence, a lived experience, and attempts to elucidate a detailed account of the nature of that experience. I look at art philosophically and address pertinent theoretical issues. But this book is not "art philosophy"; it does not formulate aesthetic definitions and categorize art works as being a certain type. Rather, it serves as a reference whereby viewers can determine for themselves the nature of artworks and how each relates to their lives.

I deal with specific philosophical concepts: transcendence, metaphysics, subjectivity, and conditionality. These terms occur frequently and are explained throughout the body of the text. I have drawn from a wide range of philosophers and do not pledge allegiance to any one above the other. I believe in a "continuous" approach to philosophy, one that recognizes all major schools of thought as having played a part in philosophical growth.

The three chapters of the discussion to follow were designed to provide different perspectives on a particular philosophical investigation: What is that occurrence which is art? In a word, this occurrence is *communication*. A brief outline of these three perspectives is appropriate.

"The Art Object" focuses on the communicative elements and the process entailed in the experience of art. It traces the artist's creative act that gives objective form to an idea, and the manner in which the viewer receives the message is by means of the object. This chapter serves as a general philosophical introduction to the remainder of the text.

"Ethics and Aesthetics" documents the various ideas which art has been used to convey. It chronicles the origin and evolution of ethics and aesthetics as they relate to each other. Later chapters give specific examples of ideas art has expressed through the ages.

"Freedom and Convention in Art" deals with the actual choices available to artists as a means of communicating their ideas. Here the discussion is composed of several short essays that deal with freedom, the emergence and development of conventions, and the ramifications of artistic choice to either submit to or resist convention.

I have tried to be as comprehensive as possible in my overview of the history of art. In each chapter the work of appropriate artists has been included. Some artists found their way into the history of ethics and aesthetics in Part Two, while others whose contributions were more central to the evolution of convention found their way into Part Three. Part One is intended to be read without specific examples in mind lest I prejudice readers in forming their own judgments. Considering the scope of my endeavor and the brevity of this work, the number of examples was kept to a minimum.

I have rendered a few philosophical verdicts concerning the manner and magnitude of the communicative process involved in the experience of art. For the most part all aesthetic verdicts are offered implicitly as a result of the philosophical approach. In short, an art form can be judged in accordance with its degree of communicability. First and foremost, I portray art as an existential experience that individuals must meet on their own terms, existential because each person comes out of the experience different from when the person went in. If not, the communicative occurrence that is art has not taken place. To the degree that any art form affects their lives, I allow readers to arrive at all aesthetic verdicts for themselves.

1

The Art Object

INTRODUCTION

Art and philosophy are always changing. They are both investigations into human nature. And as our nature is always changing, so must art and philosophy. Art and philosophy have one important difference: philosophy represents a body of knowledge that attempts to arrive at a valid explanation for the way things are. Philosophy does not lay claim to truth, but attempts to create truthful conditions if we are to acquire greater awareness. To assign a truth value to philosophy would be a misunderstanding of its changing nature. Philosophy has a relative truth to the degree that it is in comportment with the way things actually are at that time. Yesterday's philosophies do not convince us with the same compelling certainty as they once did, which raises the question as to whether things essentially remain the same while our understanding of things becomes more refined, or is reality actually changing and our philosophies along with it. The same question was addressed in the sixth century B.C.E. by Zeno of Elea, who took the former position, and Heraclitus, who held the latter. This ambiguity is part and parcel of philosophy's changing nature and is the reason why our participation in philosophy is always skeptical and passive.

Art is something entirely different. It occurs. It communicates. Art may have its materials and its body of knowledge in the form of critical interpretations, but these are just tools to be used during the communicative act performed by an individual. In order for the occurrence that is art to take place there must be the participation of at least two beings: the artist as the originator-transmitter, and the viewer as the receiver of the communicated message. Regardless of the message, all art has its own measure of truth to the degree of its communicability.

Art philosophy is of an entirely different nature from art or philosophy. Art philosophy is more on the order of an aesthetic: it formulates definitions and arrives at conclusions. Art philosophy takes a reasonable course, and like any reasonable idea it aspires to a transcendent reality beyond finite possibilities. By an ironic twist, art philosophy looses its eternal transcendent quality by appealing to the perfectability of a formula.

The philosophical attitude always allows for further questioning. Any philosophy that attempts to conceive of a perfectable movement toward an ideal is always subject to revision. If truth is within the realm of philosophy, the cardinal rule is always to maintain the questioning attitude. The truthfulness of any proposition is revealed by offering it every measure of doubt. Instead of various philosophical camps laying claim to specific territories, philosophical thought attempts to assimilate the camps into a consistent and living whole. Philosophy has evolved into a dualism of thought in accordance with the dual nature of human existence. While there can be only one reality, and not several realities side by side, we can analyze the components of reality and understand the distinct characteristics of each.

In its most general sense, this philosophical dualism can be expressed as the metaphysical polarities of *ideas* and *material*. These terms have different designations with modulations of meanings. For the terms idea-material we can substitute abstract-concrete, subject-object, spiritual-corporeal, soul-body, internality-externality. Each of these pairs refers to a different interpretation of the dual nature of humankind. For the ancient philosophers, everything in reality was seen to have attributes from both sides. For Plato the ideal was more important than the concrete in that it represented the archetype of which every concrete object was just a casual or accidental manifestation. Plato's conception of the dual nature of existence remained the prevailing philosophical idea for nearly two millennia until in the seventeenth century when René Descartes introduced consciousness as the constituting agent of reality. "I think therefore I am" became the foundation of existence. The development of this idea by other minds such as Jean-Jacques Rousseau and Immanuel Kant arrived at the complete separation of the ideal and the material, with their synthesis as the transcendental dialectic performed by consciousness. The basis of this division was the recognition of time (subjective reality) and space (objective reality) as the two irreducible components of contingent existence. The presence of these two qualities indicates the presence of human transcendence. Transcendence thus conceived is the process of becoming in existence. As we approach the question of the art object, we must keep in mind the idea of human transcendence and seek out the boundaries between the subjective and the objective because reality is comprised of qualities from these two spheres of existence in the form of metaphysical objects. The metaphysical object is subjectively crossing the threshold of objectivity.

With the introduction of consciousness as the constituting agent of our perceptions and therefore our entrance into reality, a new dualism emerged: that which presents itself to our consciousness—the subjective—as a shell around things as they actually exist in themselves—the objective. This led to a further elaboration in terms of the dual nature of humankind: consciousness-automatism, organism-environment, and freedom-nature. These are the respective terminologies adopted by psychology, behaviorism, and existentialism.

Philosophies, in their tendency toward unification, have searched for a wholistic answer to the problem of humankind's dual nature. G. W. F. Hegel described a "pure consciousness"[1] which incorporated all of history from the foundation of our being into the thickness of the immediate present. Gestalt psychology seeks psychosomatic equivalents that bridge the gap between consciousness and the automatic. There has been the natural give and take that allows for fruitful development of ideas in opposition to each other. On one side philosophies stress the subjective—transcendentalism and existentialism—on the other side, the more empirically oriented philosophies of pragmatism, positivism, and atomism.

The idea of reality being divided and that each side represents some aspect of reality which excludes the other is best exemplified in the ideas of 'being' and 'nonbeing.' The idea of a threshold, across which things come into existence, can be found in both ancient Eastern and Western philosophies, and continues to be the mainstream of twentieth-century philosophical thought. The idea of something brought forth by a negation of nonbeing will be of importance when we finally ask ourselves, "What is art?"

What is art? How do we distinguish what is art from what is not art? Is it possible for all things to be art? Or for any thing to be art? Definitions tend to be, more often than not, limitations based on predispositions or prejudices. The real problem in trying to come to a definition is that art is not a thing. Art is not something that just *is*; art is something that *occurs*. Aristotle stated his definition of art in just those terms when he said that "art is produced when out of many ideas gained through experience we come to one general conclusion."[2] Here we have a definition of art in which something occurs. Coming to a general conclusion might seem to be an arbitrary definition if it weren't for the *we*. *We* come to a conclusion. *We* agree. This community of agreement is what gives art its ethical component. However, disagreement does not nullify an object as a work of art. Rejection out of hand because of our definitions would violate our philosophical oath. Much of what art has attempted to communicate, particularly during the last two centuries, has been in the way of experimentation; and in the spirit of investigation, art lost much of its ethical character. This altered an important aspect of how art relates to our lives, that which belongs to the spiritual-subjective side.

All things in life revolve around the contradiction inherent in being and nonbeing, and we live by the law of noncontradiction: things cannot both be and not be. Still in our drive toward an absolute unity we want to bring all things under one banner, even if it results in our own annihilation, which the unity of being and nonbeing would mean. The broadest parameters of what art can be cannot escape the paradox of nonbeing. As boundaries are expanded to include all that can possibly be art, the limit of all-being is finally reached. When we can no longer allow any thing not to be art, we have arrived at an absurd contradiction; indeed, there is a philosophy of the absurd which expounds on the irrevocable differences between how we perceive and think about the world and how the world actually is.

To be as comprehensive and truthful as possible, art cannot be a matter of agreement. We must include art that we agree is art as well as that about which we disagree. We shall therefore say that art is an occurrence. The occurrence that is art, considered in its most pregnant sense, is the communication of an idea. Again we are faced with the dualism at the heart of our discussion. On the one side we have the subjective act, which is the communicative act of both the artist and the viewer, while on the other side we have the art object, which, in and of itself, does not occur, but remains as a cipher of the communication which can only be fulfilled by the presence of a subjective being. It will now be encumbent upon us to examine the aspects of the objective and subjective environment in which the art object occupies a unique place. It is hoped that through an encompassing understanding of reality, our place in that reality, and the art object's place in reality, we will be able to recognize the impact and importance to our lives of the message that the art object is communicating.

THE ART OBJECT

Every art form must communicate its particular message. When we express ourselves in language we are communicating ideas using a highly differientiated material that is formed into prose and poetry. The words are signs with specific meanings in the world. Music is also formed of materials that are expressive of emotions and impulses. Melodies rise and fall with a lyrical quality that can lift our spirits. Clashes and dissonance can convey feelings of awe and dread. There is a definite occurrence in the art forms of literature and music because the element of time is incorporated into the aesthetic experience. They unfold and progress in time. There is development of exposition that spurs our expectations. We are led down a trail to a consummation. Foreshadowing devices add to the intensity of the experience.

Art objects—e.g., paintings and sculptures—do not have this dynamic quality of unfolding and progress. The communicative message is static in time and space. Yet the object is still called upon to communicate. When the act of creation is over, the communication is not complete. The recipient must now receive the communication through the object. The materials themselves are of less importance than the manner in which the object is used to communicate the message.

Artists have something to communicate. They must shape their material to carry the message. This they do by performing the act

of giving objectified form to their ideas. This is the beginning of
the communicative process. There is a synthesis as a result of the
act, which results in an object. This synthesis of material and idea
is performed not only by human hands, but also by human transcendence. Transcendence is the process of becoming in existence.
The subjective idea has been given an enduring form, and all enduring
forms are historically determined. This does not mean that the form
is necessarily based on some historical precedent. It means that artists
bring with them the thickness of their entire past and bring it to
bear on the object. This includes the artists' personal histories as
well as the shared history of culture. The communicability of the
objects they create will depend on the manner and extent to which
there is an integration of the artists' personal histories and the shared
history or, put differently, how the artists are able to shape their
own unique experiences into an object for universal contemplation.
This is the artworks' transcendental quality. But once an object is
created and left on its own, it doesn't 'transcend.' Transcendence
is a human operation. In order for the synthesis of transcendence
to occur, there must be the presence of a living, subjective being,
a being who is always changing and stands to gain in the transaction
of self-becoming.

The object on its own can find no transcendent home. As an
object that now exists in the world in its own right it has an empirical
reality. To attribute to it a psychological reality is a misleading play
on words because it is within our subjective selves that the
psychological reality is to be found. If the existing empirical object
is capable of triggering a psychological response in us, it is because
the artwork is a subjective idea invested with objectivity through
human transcendence. We can look to the object as the carrier of
the message. Without the presence of the synthesizing power of the
subjective being, the melding of the two cannot take place.

The communicative process is not complete without the viewer.
Viewers approach the object. With them they also bring their own
historically determined subjectivity.[3] Our historically determined subjectivity is not a storehouse of historical information that we carry
in our heads, but a sense of all our past experiences condensed into
the thickness of our present selves. It is the eternal present in which
the entire thickness of the past is condensed. We think of the present
as the 'immediate.' The immediate is the one thing that all of us

have in common throughout time. One 'immediate' is mediated by the next, which is mediated by the next, and so on, to create the impression of a sequence, the record of which is history. All these immediates are contained in the thickness of the present. These immediates are our conscious reality. They constitute time itself. When we look at a work of art and identify with it, we recognize in it a part that went into the making of our immediate present. We learn something of ourselves or of our world as seen through that thickness, a part that may have otherwise gone unnoticed. We have come to a point of self understanding. The synthesis takes place in our minds, not in the object. The communicative process is then complete. The artist has presented us with a gift. In return we have received the artist into our lives with gratitude.

The art object confronts us with the same dualism that was discussed in the introduction. The empirical object-sensible and the historic object-temporal act as relay stations between different subjectivities, each unique, yet each with shared particularities. This is the art object's metaphysical definition. Then it becomes a matter of examining the communicative elements of reality to determine their presence, and thus the magnitude of the communication.

Empiricism generally refers to all things that can be verified by experience or experiment. In order for our understanding of empiricism to be as broad and encompassing as possible, we will define as empirical all things that are disclosed to our senses in addition to all things that we are capable of thinking about. We must include the workings of our consciousness because it is a part of the totality of experience. But we will not consider this totality as something actually achieved, because the most important component, the synthesizing agent of the human transcendent self, is something never fully arrived at, but always in the process of becoming something else—our future selves. This process continually extends the boundaries of the totality of reality. The totality of reality will be considered by the Jasperian term, the "encompassing."[4] The encompassing will have subsumed under it all things we defined as the empirical. These components are all coexistent and must be present and accounted for if our subjective will is to perform the synthesis of transcendence in unconditional freedom.

We first meet mundane existence, the brute reality of objectivity: rocks, trees, walls, our flesh and blood in a purely physical sense.

That which is purely physical is divorced from any reflective thought. Sensuous and tactile qualities must first be registered, and then we must be conscious of them in order to perceive this aspect of the encompassing. This leads to what seems to be an irreparable break between subject and object, as developed by transcendental realism. It states that if our access to reality is only our own cognitive capacities, then we can never truly know the nature of things-in-themselves, which creates a further dualism: on one side stand representations, which tell us more about ourselves than the real nature of objects, while on the other rests a kernel of reality that remains beyond appearances, inaccessible to our efforts at comprehending it. Consistent with the philosophical tendency toward unity, the transcendentalists did recognize the subject as the synthesizing agent of the ideal-real world; they gave the subject a motive—the search for absolutes, such as God. All divisions between the ideal and real notwithstanding, we as subjective beings are always aware of this mundane aspect of the encompassing as an "inalienable presence."

Next let us consider consciousness. It has a varied nature consisting of a consciousness-at-large and a shared consciousness. These are what allow us to communicate through communal possessions, such as language, history, and culture. But this consciousness is not our self-consciousness, namely, that part of our subjectivity which is the origin of our actions leading to self-fulfillment. Self-consciousness is the reflective self which constitutes and orients our impressions of the world and ourselves. But even this consciousness seems inadequate for many twentieth-century philosophers, primarily the existentialists, who have speculated on a prereflective consciousness. They proceed by assuming the objective world as a given, as being already there without the constituting agent of reflective consciousness. They envision a "bracketed" antepredicative world that allows for infinite predicative possibilities.[5] The existentialists view this prereflective consciousness as a necessary requirement for the process of filling out our consciousness with the content of reflective thought. This filling out is achieved by means of our understanding and intuitive capacities. The existentialists preoccupy themselves with the study of the negation of being. (The phenomenological doctrine describing reflective consciousness as "backing in" to a preexisting field of meaning is consistent with the existential claim of consciousness as the negation of being.) Psychology has also picked up on the idea of a prereflective consciousness, symbols of which it has claimed to have isolated in the subconscious mind by means of psychoanalysis.

This brings us to the concept of the understanding, which is the part of the conscious self that allows for the development of experiential knowledge. Through repetition and habituation of experiences, the understanding allows for the development of our memories and inferential logic. Our sense organs, by means of each becoming highly differentiated, integrate into a total sensory apparatus within our understanding, which thus becomes the foundation of our intuition. It is within the understanding that the world acquires an objective validity that aspires to reason.

The understanding's drive to unify the differentiated materials it finds in the world is its drive to reason. Reason is our commitment to an intersubjective truth that lies beyond all finite possibilities. Reason is a realm completely different from understanding. In it we no longer attempt to catalog all of life's manifestations; instead, we are creating a unity of them. Reason is also the seat of our spiritual being in that it attempts to conceive as one the inwardness of the self, which we might call the soul and that seemingly alien "other" of externality. It is the reasonable drive to unify the inwardness of our life with the outwardness of the world that lays the foundation for our belief in metaphysical objects.

Reason is the component of the conscious self that is pervaded by the idea. Ideas are what give form to our subjective acts. All subjective acts must find an objective home, either in concrete objects, or in objects of thought. The act of entering into a collective spiritual awareness objectifies itself in religion and civic pride. The act of performing ethical conduct objectifies itself in laws. The act of choosing between alternatives objectifies itself as freedom; the act of communicating an idea objectifies itself as an art object in the broadest sense of that term. If the idea is utilitarian, the object is of a pragmatic or industrial nature. The art in four walls is in the idea of the utility of the enclosedness within. If the idea is an attempt to give expression to our subjectivity, the object is of a metaphysical or liberal nature. Philosophy, religion, mythology, and all artworks, are metaphysical objects. It is a metaphysical object that remains as a cipher of man's transcendence. Metaphysical and created objects have one important common characteristic: their objective validity is determined by general consensus. Objective validity is simply an intersubjective stamp of approval. In this way the idea is closely associated with personality. It is the subject as personality by which the idea becomes reality.

In these aspects of human consciousness we have three levels along which our subjectivity is integrated into the objective world. First there is consciousness-at-large, followed by individual consciousness—which is now empirically defined—and finally an objective validity that aspires to unity in reason, idea, and personality. In addition, there is the last tier of being within the encompassing: that which is enclosed within the circle of the human transcendent self. It is the area where our being is always in the process of becoming, always *en route*. While being on the empirical level may be finite at any one particular time, transcendent being is capable of infinite possibilities within the temporal flux. By means of our projects we create a future for ourselves. By enacting those projects we surpass them and become that future self, now laying the foundation for future projects. In order to enact this self-becoming, all of these previous modes of the encompassing must be present. The denial, suppression, or favoring of any one will depreciate the overall unity of truthfulness. Without total disclosure we cannot be complete or free. This is the essense of our being. We bring our possibilities to fruition and something new and unprecedented is created, but we can only do so if we are free. The essential truth of human becoming in existence is freedom. Freedom is engendered as we become our projected selves. This is why Søren Kierkegaard said, "Truth is subjectivity."6

Only in the presence of the totality of the encompassing can we act in an environment of freedom; indeed, freedom is the product of the act. If a man is denied anything, he cannot be totally sure that his actions will ensure the unconditionality of self-becoming. The unconditional act is that which allows him to become what he chooses. The object of the unconditional act is the projected self. Without access to the totality of alternatives and possibilities his actions cannot be totally free. A conditional act is therefore one which is not of the nature of bringing about self-becoming, but is made to fulfill some other condition.

The creative act of the artist is always unconditional. Once the creative act is complete an artist becomes new and different. The communicative act of an artist can be either conditional or unconditional. However, because the communicative act is not complete until it has been received, the act's conditionality is determined upon acceptance by the perceiver. The communicative act is conditional when the perceiver's acceptance of its cipher—the object—never gets beyond understanding. In other words, our intellect can understand the idea being communicated, but it tells us nothing about ourselves. The perceiver receives the communicative act unconditionally as a gift of self-knowledge. The artist receives in return the enduring nature of his idea and personality as a part of our lives. In this way the artist's act is nothing short of a quest for immortality. The breadth of the encompassing will determine the artist's success. It is the encompassing that supplies the material, and the transcendent self that provides the focus for this phenomenon of human existence.

This schemata of the encompassing is just that, a facsimile, just as descriptions in and of themselves are not the things they describe. But they provide a framework in which all creations can find their place. All communicative ideas have their empirical reality, whether or not the ideas are objectified in media of representation. The idea of freedom is objectified in the act of choice, which must necessarily be a choice between things either concrete or abstract. While all objects have a place within the schemata of a situation where freedom is engendered by the act of choosing, we would not say that freedom is a quality of the objects, but the end result of a synthesis performed by the individual.

We have an empirical object with an immediate presence in the world; it is a cipher for the communicative act—the communication of an idea. The artist has given it sensible qualities, and it has a historical orientation. The power of the idea will be determined by the level at which two perspectives of space and time (sensory and historical) are integrated into a reasonable whole, a vision of a transcendent reality that fuses the particular with the universal.

The message of the artist is now something real in the world. But the transmission and reception of the message is not something that the art can perform on its own. It must first have the active transmitter—the artist—and then the active receptor/perceiver—the viewer. The object stands as a cipher, or mediator, of the subjective idea. The idea was once immediate with the act of the artist, and the object, too, remains immediate. But once the idea is given concrete form, the act is no longer immediate. It must be performed again in the immediate by the viewer. Our immediate relation to the empirical object is the same as the artist's immediate relation: we bring the same sensory and historic interpretations to it. But once the viewer has performed the receptive end of the communication, the idea is now twice removed from the subjective act of the artist. The object is itself a facsimile of the idea, and our perceptions of the object are again a reassembling of the idea as it is integrated by our own spacio-temporal orientation. An understanding of this encompassing totality will help clarify in our minds the artist's gift of communication.

Any artwork that asks for blind acceptance of its idea is a denial of full disclosure, and as such lacks truth. Such art becomes estranged from the unity of reality as it finds comfort in the backwaters of a mundane intellectualism where demands are not made, only explanations offered and accepted. Artists who demand that we learn something about ourselves through their creations have made an unconditional demand. Our subjective self in the world is the object of the communicative act. This is the transcendental synthesis of subject and object. The only condition is that of self-becoming, which is never of a finite or perfectable nature, but is always open to further possibilities, subject as our lives are to the continual flux of existence.

NOTES

1. Georg W. F. Hegel, "The Phenomenology of the Spirit," *The Philosophy of Hegel* (New York: Modern Library, 1954), pp. 410–34.
2. Aristotle, *Metaphysics* (New York: Walter J. Black, 1943), Bk. 1, chap. 1, p. 6.
3. Martin Heidegger, "The End of Philosophy and the Task of Thinking," *Basic Writings* (New York: Harper and Row, 1976), pp. 380–82.
4. Karl Jaspers, *Philosophy* (Chicago: University of Chicago Press, 1970). Jaspers' use of the term, "encompassing," to describe the totality of existence is found throughout most of his books.
5. Edmund Husserl, *General Introduction to Pure Phenomenology* (New York: Collier Books, 1962), #31, p. 96.
6. Søren Kierkegaard, *Concluding Unscientific Postscript* (Princeton: Princeton University Press, 1941), p. 169.

2

Ethics and Aesthetics

INTRODUCTION

Ethics and aesthetics share a common origin. When primitive humans carved their idols and performed their rituals, it was an attempt to shape and tame the terrifying and destructive forces of nature before which they found themselves trembling. It was a making of order out of chaos. Because they were taking a world they found inadequate to their needs and reshaping it according to how it *ought* to be, these first stirrings of humankind's sense of its place in the world were the beginning of ethics.

Ethics began with the recognition that all people share something in common. All are here in the immediate present. We all coexist in the objective world, and we share a bond with our fellow beings in a spiritual sense that manifests itself in love, respect, admiration, and loyalty. As people gathered together and formed societies, the recognition of these shared properties lead to the development of the central concern of ethics—how do people live together?

Ethics consists of standards of conduct to guide human behavior. All artworks that were produced prior to the Renaissance were created as vehicles of some explicit ethical message. Whether they were hieroglyphics glorifying the military prowess of a pharaoh, a Greek drama exemplfying the virtues of heroism, or Gothic statues adorning the portals of a cathedral, they were all created as an appeal for people to conduct themselves in a certain way. Our collective ethical awareness can be most easily identified in the form of religion and civic pride.

Artifacts of the neolithic period are a record of human's first becoming self-conscious. Man no longer scampered about on all fours looking down at the earth. He looked up and saw himself in relation to the world. He experienced the rhythm of life in the cycle of the seasons and saw order in the cosmos with the return of the equinox. With his new awareness of his place in the cosmos neolithic man began to think about his world. His reasoning—however primitive—arrived at the transcendental reality of god, the absolute by which all was possible.

The world was also a place of disorder. The sun and stars remained fixed while the planets made their way across the sky in an irregular manner. These heavenly bodies were ascribed with supersensible qualities wielding magical power over the lives of humans. Natural disasters were attributed to supernatural demons. A pantheon of gods, both good and evil, were conjured.

These gods were symbolic of different characteristics of the human psychological make-up. The bad gods were manifestations of early man's deepest fears and horrors. The good gods were symbolic of his hopes and aspirations, his desire for a community in which all would live in agreement and harmony. These gods were representations of a system of ethics, assimilated into their culture as religious doctrines and secular codes, and objectified in all manner of idols and icons.

All of these laws, doctrines, and images were conceived as reconciliation of prehistoric man's inwardness and spirit with the great externality of the world in all of its horrifying and comforting totality. As metaphysical objects they gave people a definite sense of place in the world. This sense of a relationship to the world is best given concrete shape in early man's creation of the art object. Here is an object in the real world, loaded with symbolic representations of impulses from deep within the human psyche. It is a confrontation of the mystery of life, and the drive to conquer that mystery.

The origins of nationalism and civic pride predate the rise of cities and states, and were already objects of conscious awareness and concern with the emergence of the first true social communities during the fourth millennium B.C.E. The origin of developing cities, and thus civic pride, can be traced to the moment when primitive men stopped being hunter-gatherers, grouped together, and developed an agrarian way of life. Of primary importance was the achievement of a surplus of production. This allowed much of the labor force to conduct other activities such as trade, administration, and warfare. thus creating more proud and mighty nations.

Religion also became aligned with, and in the service of, the state. The ruling monarch's authority on earth was believed to be the work of the gods, and indeed kings and queens were deemed godly themselves in their capacity to conquer and to administer justice. In the depiction of these earliest god-kings (circa 3000 B.C.E.) there is never any doubt who the king is. He is invariably "larger than life," and being assisted by supernatural spirits. Most impressive of these early monuments to the priest-king is the stele of Hammurabi (1760 B.C.E.); on which it shows the king being handed the code of justice directly from the sun god.

Artists and scribes became important individuals in the society, their job being the glorification and immortalization of the king. Between the king and the artisans there arose a class of priests and religious men who counselled the king in other-worldly matters. The priests instructed him on the proper performance of sacrificial rituals, augured the entrails of animals for divine revelations, and generally appealed to the gods for auspicious circumstances. These soothsayers and oracles instructed artists and craftsmen in the construction of temples, idols, and ceremonial artifacts. The priests directed all of society in the adoration of the king, the gods, and the state.

The means to represent ethical ideas became more differentiated and refined. Advancements were made in techniques and materials, and by way of practice and custom, aesthetics evolved. The development of aesthetics has also been the product of agreement. Certain representations were deemed appropriate concatenations of spiritual communion with fellow humans and with beings from the spiritual world. Certain images and symbols became common property by virtue of the power the ethical proscriptions held on society. In this way aesthetics can be viewed as a form of ethics.

All development of aesthetics in the visual arts—the sculpture of classical Greece, the painting of the Flemish masters, and in all of architecture—was achieved as a means of giving greater clarity of expression to ethical aspirations. Art was in the service of ethics, and the artist was subservient to the prevailing aesthetics. We know the names of the sculptors of ancient Greece. When we look at their work, we get a fused version of their personalities, fused to the ideal of which their contributions were just one link in the process. The strength of their personalities was absorbed into the ideal. Yet the artists do gain a measure of self-fulfillment by giving the ideal a broader and deeper significance.

During the millennium that witnessed the spread of Christianity across Europe, the years that coincide with the Byzantine, Romanesque and Gothic epochs, aesthetics continued its devoted service to ethics. This was the age of faith when absolution was sought in the eternal light of God's heavenly community. Aesthetics became a strict program elucidating the proper ethical conduct that would lead to ultimate redemption. The artisans working during these years created in even greater anonymity than their ancient counterparts, yet their work, as a collective effort, strives to express a more narrowly defined absolute—the one and only God and its absolute necessity.

The beginning of the modern age in art can be defined as that time at which the individuality of artists began to assert itself. This dramatic break of ethics and aesthetics coincides with the historical period known as the Renaissance, which viewed the individuality of the person and the artist with greater importance. This was brought about by a combination of circumstances. First, rediscovery of the philosophers of antiquity gave Renaissance man a whole new perspective on his place in the universe. Second, the abuses of the church, most notably by the notorious Borgia pope Alexander VI, turned many people away from the institution that was supposed to be their spiritual home. And finally, progress in commerce and science created an environment in which the unique character and strength of the human personality could find full expression.

This was the age of discovery. The age of Leonardo, Copernicus, and Galileo. The rediscovery of ancient philosophers and men of science revolutionized the way people of the time thought about the world. The reintroduction of humanism placed within the capacity of persons the ability to understand and reason about the nature of the universe, even if their abilities were still attributable to the grace of Divine will. To question man's Earthly path as a means of righting oneself on the eternal path to God's glory was the great contribution to humanism achieved in Dante's (1265–1321) epic poem *The Divine Comedy*. The ethical constraints imposed by religion still maintained authority over people's lives, but a radical change had taken place. In 1517, when Martin Luther nailed his list of grievances against the papacy on the door of the church in Wittenberg, and thus initiated the Protestant Reformation, it brought into question the doctrines and practices of the Catholic Church. It asserted that each person held within his own heart the manner in which to express his faith in God.

With a heightened awareness of the world came an increased interest in human history. The relics of the past were no longer looked upon only as plunder to be hoarded, but as objects to behold in wonder upon the condition of his past, and therefore himself. It was only after the Renaissance that institutions resembling museums first came into existence. Perhaps the first museum was that of Lorenzo di Medici, which housed not only artifacts, but also artists, poets, and philosophers. Gathered in his collection were the humanist poet Angelo Poliziano, the neo-Platonist Marsilio Ficino, and the sculptor Michelangelo.

This new environment in which the art object was placed and scrutinized represented a radical change in the way art was looked at and thought about. By taking the art object out of its context and placing it on a pedestal our comprehension is no longer as that of the person who created them as symbols to live by. Removing the object from its original purpose and analyzing it, we may arrive at rationalizations that would be completely alien to the artist, or the audience for which the art work was intended. Inevitably, the creation of a "museum space" also created a demand to replenish that space with ever new artistic sensations. And it is in this new context in which we find the genesis of the phrase "art for art's sake." Art was no longer only an expression of man's ethical needs. Aesthetics had taken on a life of its own. If art still made the effort to convey the ethical community of God, it must take a back seat to art as the expression of the power of man's mind. This did not mean that aesthetics was no longer concerned with conveying ethical communion. The spirit of investigation born in the Renaissance changed the nature of ethics and aesthetics, it did not destroy it. The ethical message implicitly became the sharing of ideas about the world. There was still the element of agreement: what art was attempting to convey had to be understood and accepted.

The Renaissance raised the stature of the artist to that of a celebrity. Raphael (1485–1520) and Michelangelo Buonarrotti (1475–1564) lived like royalty, and in the north of Europe, Flemish painter

Jan Van Eyck (1370–1440) and German painter Hans Holbein (1465?–1524) were rewarded with royal commissions. But not all great artists were recognized in their time, and for every artist fortunate enough to find wealthy patrons, there were many more living in abject poverty. This new role of the artist as personality also gave rise to an ever changing view of aesthetics. Before the Renaissance, art was produced in accordance with a program that categorized what we would call the style of the period. Later, artists had to contend with being either in or out of style, or more properly put, in or out of fashion. When Botticelli (1447?–1515) painted *The Birth of Venus* in 1480, he was the "toast" of Florence. Twenty years later he could not find commissions, yet his former student Filipino Lippi (1457–1504) was heralded as the "darling" of the art world.

The sixteenth century was witness to the first full flowering of the artist as a unique personality. It was the classical ideal, developed during the Renaissance, that provided the resistance against which the genius of Michelangelo and the Venetian painter Titian (1477?–1576) were able to assert themselves. Titian occupied a pivotal position in the dramatic new role that painting was to assume. Before Titian, all painting was still in the service of God and country, unable to break free of conventional and acceptable modes of representation. *What* was represented was of primary concern; *how* it was represented was simply in accordance with art's didactic purpose. With Titian we see the first real concern with *how* subjects were represented. Before Titian painting was a craft, and while many masters gave great depth of expression to their art, it is with Titian that the art of painting was born. Titian gave us a view of the world that goes beyond the message contained in the content of the picture. His work tells us something new about the world and its purpose is not to instruct but to share. Titian has presented us with a gift, an awareness of being in the world. This gift to humankind is of greater importance to the art of painting. It freed the artist to find his potential, and the towering genius of Titian shines eternally in that continuing quest.

By the turn of the seventeenth century, painting had become big business complete with commercial picture salons and art dealers. Paintings became commodities, and demand for all types of subject matter rose: landscapes, still-lifes, portraits, genre scenes, historical scenes, seascapes, nocturnes, interiors, and many others. The proliferation and diversification of artistic production naturally lead to the development of various schools with their own aesthetic programs. The academies of the "art establishment" pursued a conventional technique coupled with a strict doctrine of acceptable subject matter, most notably history and religion. In any field where certain individuals are favored by a coterie of official tastemakers, the outsiders, or "have nots," team in opposition. Fermenting on the fringe of the artistic world were rebels and innovators who, instead of following preestablished doctrines, were interested in developing their powers of observation, and with their imaginations extending the limits of the potential of painting as a medium.

In the seventeenth century, scientific progress, particularly that of optics, gave the artist new areas to explore. This field was lead by the Dutch. Painters of city streets and homey interiors displayed an enhanced acuity in the depiction of microscopic detail. The Dutch landscape painters mimicked every conceivable atmospheric condition, and Jan Vermeer (1632–1675) created a dazzling new gem-like quality to his paintings, aided by the optical device known as the *camera obscura.**

The term "baroque" still contains associations of its original meaning of being irregular and arcane, a denigrating comparison with the classical ideal. Indeed, the painters of the seventeenth and eighteenth centuries did pursue an irregular course into esoteric domains. With the coming of the Enlightenment (generally considered to be between 1688 and 1789) and the revival of pagan philosophy, a total deterioration of any consistent aesthetic was complete. Artists vied for attention by decking out their paintings with an extravaganza of allegoric effluence. Yet, at the same time, while painting as a whole foundered for lack of direction, the situation was such that the power of the artist's personality was nurtured. Success made artists world renowned and brought along all the egotism and professional rivalries that generally attend success. And with the right individual, given the right circumstances, geniuses the magnitude of a Jean Baptiste Chardin (1699–1779), a Francisco Guardi (1712–1793), or a Francisco Goya (1746–1828), rose above the mediocrity of their age to leave us a record of a time that speaks clearly because it has captured

---

*A darkened box in which the image of an object enters a small opening via a lens and is projected in natural color on a plane surface where it can be viewed, traced, or photographed.

the history upon which we have raised ourselves. But no genius is of the rank to sustain a style in dissolution. The tributaries of the baroque style, instead of flowing into a unified body, branched out into obscure backwaters. Aesthetics began to fragment because it no longer had ethical guidance and control. In natural opposition to this trend was the gravitation toward the comfortable and reassuring rigidity of the classical ideal as exemplified in the neoclassicism of Jacques Louis David (1748–1826) and Jean Auguste Ingres (1780–1867). By the same token, the dynamic brilliance of Eugène Delacroix (1799–1863) and the romantics could never have asserted itself and found expression had there not been the rigid neoclassical doctrine against which to rebel. Art seemed to be charging hysterically in opposite directions.

The nineteenth century was to see the true flowering of "art for art's sake." By the 1840s Gustave Courbet (1819–1877) had introduced a new, and at the time shocking, realism. John Constable (1776–1837) and Jean Corot (1796–1875) painted with a new naturalism in their approach to landscape, and Frederick Jackson Turner (1861–1932) was already the precursor to impressionism. By mid-century Jean François Millet (1814–1875) and Honoré Daumier (1808–1879) brought social consciousness to the fore in painting, and by the 1860s the idea of a spontaneous perception of light as the operative of color gave birth to impressionism.

Progress in science and technology during the nineteenth century brought about a radical change in the world and these changes would necessarily affect art. Developments in communication by rail, steamer, and wire had made the world a much smaller place, and the artists had a multitude of new subjects and concerns with which to deal. The invention of photography brought about a complete reevaluation of the role and technique of painting. Physics had bestowed animation on what had been considered inert matter, and the rise of the psychoanalytic profession gave the artist another new domain to discover—the cavernous recesses of the human conscious and subconscious mind.

By the late nineteenth century, although there was still an official line held by the academies and *l'ecole des beaux-arts,* the idea of a consistent and agreed upon form of expression was gone forever. The academies still flourished, but alongside new salons dedicated to the discoverers of light, the Impressionists. The proliferation of new artistic ideas found ready and willing adherents, each vying for recognition and acclaim. The symbolists pursued a deep metaphoric meaning in their work as a key to the adumbrations of the soul. The Pre-Raphaelites looked back to the origins of the Renaissance classics for guidance, and in such disparate locales as Arles, Tahiti, and Norway, a raw expressionistic vitality would find its outlet in the work of Vincent van Gogh (1853–1890), Paul Gauguin (1848–1903), and Edvard Munch (1863–1944). And yet the fragmentation of the art world in the late nineteenth century was a mere pretext to what would follow.

At the beginning of the twentieth century an explosion of different artistic trends took place that was unprecedented in the history of art. Post-impressionism, cubism, futurism, suprematism, abstraction, Dada, surrealism, expressionism, as well as the work of the academies, all had their own followings during the first quarter of the century. The remainder of the century has only seen an acceleration of the same. Today there are individuals who are considered art movements in and of themselves. Individuality has come to be the sole criteria of art. How has this development affected art and the ideas that art tries to communicate? The following sections will describe how ideas and personality have influenced art, and the effect that the ascendance of personality has had on ethics and aesthetics.

THE PRIMITIVES

The consciousness of the primitive mind was not as differentiated and refined as that of modern humans, and the primitives' earliest attempts to reconcile their inwardness and spirit with the great externality of the world were simple and direct. The primitive mind had a limited self-awareness, or ego, against a vast repository of the subconscious self. These two parts of the self were in constant combat. The ego, in its form of objectified self in the world attempts to appropriate as its own all that it encounters. The unconscious self infringes upon the domain of the ego, subjecting it to fear and doubt brought about by the vague awareness of there being something more, something beyond, that our conscious self was unable to grasp and make its own. The art object, or idol, was then called upon to bridge these two spheres of the human mind and give meaning to this elusive and spiritual side of human nature. This is the object's metaphysical duty.

Some of the best evidence of pre-historic man's incursions into the supernatural are preserved in the caves at Lascaux in the south of France. These primitives had a sensitivity to the organic form of their subjects that was seldom equaled. With our modern sensibilities and developed mental capacities we can still feel the magic that surrounds these figures. They were created as incarnations of the forces hidden behind nature. The depictions of fertile bulls and cows fat with calf were appeals for providential provisions. It is curious how primitive artists did not display the same ability in rendering the human figure as they did the animal; this would seem to be a direct indication of their low self-consciousness against an abundant subconscious yet real world that was the object of their spiritual concerns. Because it weighed so heavily on their consciousness, the spiritual world was more real for the primitive than for the modern mind, thus the primitive's was permeated by a more meaningful spirituality.

How did these primitive objects acquire their meanings for the primitive mind? In any interpretation of the metaphysical synthesis of humankind and its world there must be interpreters who are able to divine and give these objects spiritual significance. In primitive societies (and still in contemporary primitive cultures) the role of interpreter was assumed by the shaman—a priest, magician, medicine man, or wizard.

The shaman was both venerated and feared. He might be called upon to perform a number of different magical rituals: the incantation of good spirits and the chasing away of evil ones, the healing of the sick, or the divining of the spiritual forces lurking behind natural phenomena. The shaman had a financial agreement with the tribal chief: he would accumulate tributes from the members of the tribe who curried his favor, and these he would share with the chief. In return the chief would give the shaman unquestioned authority as the sole source of supernatural explanations.

The shaman was more than just a powerful medicine man who held his position through the authority of the chief. By today's standards we might say he had psychic or clairvoyant qualities. Certainly he had an acute sensitivity to the emotional substrata of the primitive mind. In many cases the shaman displayed a neuroticepileptoid character, prone to fits and hallucinations. The epileptoid was viewed as possessing miraculous self-healing powers by delivering himself from delirium and sickness back to health. The shaman was able to recognize the power his odd behavior had over the tribe and thereby manipulate its effects to strengthen his position.

THE ANCIENT WORLD

The Greek city-state must be considered a work of art itself. Every aspect of life was directed toward the regulation of the state, and every man had his place in the hierarchy. The Greek mind had developed significantly since paleolithic men carved images on cave walls. The Greeks had a self-awareness of their place in the cosmos, an awareness which was governed by a cosmic resignation. They viewed life as a continuous cycle of birth, death, and rejuvenation in which man was the microscopic representative of the universe. This sense of man's presence in the universe was a catalyst to the Greek mind. Never before or since has any civilization seen such a flowering of humanity: in philosophy, science, sculpture, architecture, and drama, each enhancing the environment and nurturing each other, to the point where being a citizen was an aesthetic experience.

The development of aesthetics proper—i.e., the classical ideal in sculpture, the mechanics of tragedy and comedy in literature— was regulated to embellish the ultimate art work, namely, the state. The ideal state was the topic of concern in Plato's *Republic,* and Platonic idealism was the basis of all artistic production. The monuments that adorned the Acropolis, the Greek comedies and tragedies, and above all their pantheon of Gods, were all representations of eternal truths.

One of the best illustrations of this relationship of ethics and aesthetics is the Orestian Trilogy of Aeschylus (525–456 B.C.E.). Here the ethical concepts of honor, betrayal, retribution, and ultimate justice are given full range of expression. The three-play cycle is formal and polished in structure. The first deals with betrayal, the second with revenge, and the last with justice. Literary devices enhance the dramatic affect. Choruses elucidate a consensus on ethical values, and pathos is established for a son wrongly accused. Yet these aesthetic devices are only means in establishing a higher ethical message that provides the scaffolding upon which the aesthetic components take shape. The aesthetics are ennobled through the ethical edification, rising to complement them in grandeur and power.

This relation between ethics and aesthetics can also be applied to the development of sculpture and architecture. The great centers of power—the Acropolis, Delphi, and Olympia—were embodiments of the Greeks' ethical concepts. It was aesthetics aspiring to the loftiness of their ethical ideals that brought forth the great advance in the ideal representation of the human form. The gods in the pedimental sculptures were depicted acting out heroics of virtue. The temples and treasuries were all erected in the name of loyalty and honor.

Because ancient artifacts are permeated by their ethical content, they stand as historical documents. The history of pre-Renaissance art is a record of civilization. The same cannot be said of all post-Renaissance art. However, since our understanding of these artifacts is not on the same lived, experiential level as the Greeks themselves, we fail to grasp the manner in which these objects made explicit their relation to the Greek mind. We stand in awe of their heightened aesthetic awareness and contemplate the classical era of Greece as a Parnassus of poets, philosophers, and artists living the pastoral existence of the goat herd. In reality the classical age was one of constant warfare and strife. All of the Greeks' achievements in the malleable arts, literature, philosophy, and science were developed as means of asserting the end of Greek domination and supremacy, a testament to their superiority that ultimately had to be decided on the battlefield. Alexander the Great (357–323 B.C.E.), a student of Aristotle, is still considered the greatest conqueror of all time, whose exploits are marveled at and whose tactical innovations are emulated to this day. Alexander was likened to a god. All Greek civilization, indeed the entire known world at the time, paid hommage and tribute to him.

The decay of Alexander's world during the Hellenistic period set the stage for the power that was to become Rome. The Romans were a different, coarser lot. Alexander would assimilate his territories by placing natives in command, and enjoyed decking himself and his entourage in Persian and other exotic fineries. The Romans were true occupiers, with an expansive bureaucracy for administering their provinces. All roads led to Rome, and when in Rome you did as the Romans.

Rome's sense of civic pride was based on power, and aesthetics continued to be the vehicle for giving expression to the ethics of the noble Roman. Society during the Roman Republic became highly stratified, with patricians, aristocratic landholders, civil bureaucrats, wealthy merchants, soldiers, and plebeians (the working class). While much of Roman art merely followed the Greek example, portraiture gained in importance as an expression of the power and durability of the individual and, by implication, the power of the state. During the Roman period cults formed around powerful personalities, a clear indication of the further development of humankind's ego consciousness.

To be Roman was to live an aesthetic experience all facets of which were designed for the maintenance and survival of the Roman way of life. Cato (234–149 B.C.E.), the founder of Latin prose, ended every speech with the words, "Carthage must be destroyed!" Carthage was the Roman Republic's most noteworthy economic and military rival. During the Third Punic War (148 B.C.E.) Carthage was destroyed; its people and culture completely obliterated from the face of the earth. Roman power, as republic and then empire, would endure for 500 years until the sociopolitical ramifications of a changing world would herald the inevitable uncertainty of fate.

THE AGE OF FAITH

In 313 C.E. the Emperor Constantine proclaimed Christianity as the official religion of the Roman Empire. Constantine moved his capital to Constantinople, and the division of his empire into East and West was the first act that culminated two centuries later in the birth of the Byzantine Empire. The Byzantines at first borrowed the aesthetic vocabulary of their predecessors, only the content illustrated Christian values rather than pagan ones. But the dramatic break from pagan to Christian would have social ramifications that aesthetics could not escape.

The dissolution of the ancient world would bring about the foundation of the medieval world. The first Christians were ascetics. Persecuted for their faith, they were forced to live in catacombs and as hermits in caves. Their art was introspective. Their message was devotion to the new Christian ethic and the dogmas of the church.

In time Christianity drew many new adherents and great religious centers grew in Egypt and Syria. The Christian church became the authority and spiritual spearhead pointing toward a hostle and heathen Europe. However, the real threat to Christianity was to come from another direction—the Islamic uprising of the seventh century. Secular and religious authorities would now tend to merge. Ethics and aesthetics would once again enjoy the patronage of the religious and state institutions. Art would develop totally in keeping with the new Christian ideals.

In the year 800 Charlemagne (742–814) was crowned first Holy Roman Emperor. Charlemagne was a scholar and a patron of the arts who reintroduced Latin as the official ecclesiastical language throughout his domain. This was Europe's first rediscovery of classical antiquity. It would also be the beginning of a split within the Church between East and West. In the East, orthodoxy and iconoclasm prevailed: idolatrous images were forbidden, representations of the Christ and Virgin were strictly prohibited. The Eastern church only gradually broke free of these proscriptions. Artistic emphasis was on the decorative, and exquisite works were produced in mosaic, textile design, and inlaid jewelry. In the West, art was viewed as a tool to educate the laity about the word of God. Artworks and images were not considered idols to be worshipped but illustrations of the ethical virtues of Christianity. The Western church would inevitably be responsible for the creation of all the great religious art of the Gothic, Renaissance, and baroque periods.

This pedagogical function reserved for art developed hand in hand with theological doctrine. Of paramount importance to this development is the figure of Abbot Suger of Saint-Denis (1080–1151). Suger spent sixty of his seventy years at Saint-Denis during which time he became the most influential cleric in all of France.

Suger's years at Saint-Denis represent the height of European monasticism, the system by which Christian authority was disseminated to the laity. Monastaries were the repositories of the faith in the form of sacred manuscripts. Suger was fluent in all of the important theological documents, and particularly those of Pseudo-Dionysus, the Aerogagite. Suger would develop his own neo-Platonic ideas, which would influence not only art but also religion and the state for centuries after his death. Stated simply, Suger was able to intellectualize spiritual salvation through the material world by virtue of its created existence. The material world could point in a symbolic sense to the invisible reality of the Divine world because material existence was by God's grace. The entire cosmic symbolism was displayed materially by the figure of the Christ: in his crucifixion, resurrection, and ascension.

Suger built the church at Saint-Denis as the material embodiment of his spiritual ideas. The massive structure that seems to soar and reach for Heaven is itself a metaphor for God's grace on Earth. Every doorjamb, every wall, every nook and cranny is adorned with instructive depictions from the New Testament. The Abbey at St. Denis was the first to accumulate a vast treasure of jewel-encrusted chalaces and septors. Suger reasoned that for what greater purpose could materialism be pursued than for the greater glory of God. Suger's church design, especially his stained glass windows, would set the example that Gothic structures would strive for three centuries to imitate.

GOD AS ETHICAL COMMUNITY

We may believe in God as the wholeness of ethical community without believing in Him as a personal God. God can he considered the ultimate and most exulted idea that humankind can have of itself: unconditional love for ones fellow man. Conversely, human beings can be considered the flawed images of that perfect God—this way of thinking leads to guilt.

The idea of ethical community must be arrived at by consensus. It is a leveling of all people to parity and equality. Ethics serves as the counterpoint to the brute that dwells within us. It is the security of being a part of the whole. The reasonable component of the idea of ethical community aspires to the harmonious and peaceful co-existence of all people, to the One, to God. The history of humankind is a record of the struggle between these pairs of opposites that comprise human nature. On the one side there is the brute, the instinct to dominate; it is the assertion of our subjective nature in the objective world. On the other side is the transcendent reality of God as the wholeness of ethical community, the recognition of strength and security in solidarity between human beings.

It is much easier for people to assert their subjectivity than to passively offer it up. To assert is to appropriate for one's self. To offer is to sacrifice of one's self. This psychological drama that has been played out during the course of civilization is most tellingly brought to realization in the figure of Christ. If we consider His supernatural attributes metaphorically, then the miraculous conception becomes the symbol of the birth of spiritual love, a birth not incumbent upon the machinations of the flesh. The crucifixion becomes the symbol of the sacrifice of one's self for the good of human spiritual well-being. Interpreted this way, Christ becomes the symbol of a higher spiritual evolution, attainable by all people, and indeed this is why Christ is called the Son of Man.

Sacrifice is difficult when spirituality is the reward. We find pleasure in our earthly possessions and, conversely, unhappiness in their absence. Spirituality is kept bouyant by our faith in our ethical ideas, and as the transcendental idea of God is something that we participate in and grow with, it can only come from within our transcendent selves. Sin, guilt, and eternal damnation are all coercive measures externally applied to those who lack faith in their own ethical ideals. They can only lead to a false god, not the God we carry within ourselves. One does not make a true sacrifice when enticed with heavenly rewards. True sacrifice is made here and now with the realization of what is gained here and now.

VENICE

The Venetian Republic endured for a millennium that witnessed the rise and fall of other great powers. The institution of the doge* as secular and ecclesiastic authority was the focal point around which all activities rallied. By virtue of its strategic location between East and West, and its watery tradition of raising itself upon sandbars and bogs, Venice became the great maritime trading nation of the Middle Ages. During the sixteenth and seventeenth centuries Venice was the most formidable bulwark against Turkish expansion.

Venice's unique political situation gave rise to an environment of independence and freedom. Modern Venice still resounds with the nostalgia of its former glory down every side street and canal.

*The elected chief magistrate.

St. Marks Square with its colonnade enclosure flanked by the palace of the doge and the Basilica, and overlooked by the disproportionately large watchtower, is an immortal symbol of impregnability.

The art of painting in oils owes a debt of gratitude to Venice. The Venetians were the first painters of the Renaissance to cultivate the technique of oil painting. The independent Venetians were to initiate a tradition in painting of consistently exploiting the potentials of the oil medium. Bellini, Giorgione, Titian, Tintoretto, Tiepolo, and Guardi are only a few of the Venetians whose contributions are the very pillars of the art of painting. This tradition spread far beyond Venice and continues to do so. While the capital of the "contemporary" art world has shifted from Rome to London to Paris to New York, Venice will always remain the capital of great painters.

LANDSCAPE

Landscape painting is a direct reflection of our attitude toward the environment. Prior to the Renaissance, landscape merely served as a backdrop against which the drama of the narrative content was played. During the age of discovery, painters took a new interest in representing natural forms. Leonardo da Vinci's notebooks are filled with studies from nature, and there is a veiled mystery in the depths of the landscapes that serve as background for his figure paintings. In Venice, Titian's new use of light—sketchy, flickering brushstrokes of paint—introduced the *plein-aire* (literally "open air") technique of local color that varied the color of objects when in proximity to objects of another color. In the North of Europe, under the pen of Albrecht Durer (1471–1528), humble field flowers and weeds were transformed into majestic and noble expressions of human curiosity about nature.

Great landscapes have been captured throughout the history of painting. As new artistic ideas spread across Europe, artists from all over began to take a new interest in landscape. Talents as different in temperament and style as the Brueghels,* Casper David Friedrich (1774–1840), and John Constable (1776–1837), are conspicuous for their penetrating observations and their ability to convey an eternal weightiness that boarders on the reverent.

---

*A family of Flemish painters including Pieter the Elder (c. 1525–1569).

There have been two great epochs when landscape painting rose to great heights. The first was the era of Dutch baroque landscape in the middle of the seventeenth century. This was the period immediately after the Dutch wrestled their freedom from the Spanish Hapsburgs, a period of unrivaled Dutch expansion in commerce and trade. Dutch landscape paintings were emblems of Dutch pride. They depict the land conquered, cultivated, and controlled. Every conceivable landscape type found expression due to this new civic pride. The feeling and power of these landscapes boarder on a godly adoration that has a transcendent quality that goes far beyond the mere geography.

The second great epoch of landscape painting is that known as the Hudson River School of nineteenth-century America. Here we are also dealing with a period following national independence and rapid territorial expansion. Starting with the Hudson River Valley, these painters gradually filtered west as the country grew in that direction. The entire country was consumed by the idea of manifest destiny—that the United States was destined to occupy the North American continent from coast to coast—and American landscape painters depicted their homeland with a reverence that was akin to their Dutch counterparts of two centuries earlier. It must be remembered that these American painters were mostly trained in Europe, in the artistic centers of London, Dusseldorf, and Rome. There is little doubt that when they returned to their homeland, they saw the American landscape with "European eyes."

AMERICAN POSTSCRIPT

The American sense of civic pride also found expression through architecture. The United States was a product of the Enlightenment, that flurry of philosophical speculation during the eighteenth century. Our founding fathers were steeped in the political philosophies of Thomas Hobbs and John Locke, who were themselves influenced by the philosophers of antiquity. In search of a national style that paid hommage to their classical roots, American architects adopted the Greek Revival. In 1789, George Washington was sworn in as the first President of the United States on the steps of what could only be described as a modern Greek temple—the building in New

York City which is known today as Federal Hall National Monument. Greek Revival became the fashionable style particularly for stately Southern mansions during the neoclassical era (c. 1820).

BEAUTY

> "When all the world knows beauty as beauty, then ugliness comes into being."
>
> —Lao Tzu

The aesthetic value of beauty has had a greater affect on artistic production than any other value. Beauty has been persistently pursued as an ideal worthy of artistic attainment. Not surprisingly, no other aesthetic value has been as misunderstood and, consequently, none has been subjected to as much unwarranted denegation or praise.

Beauty as an ideal is the assimilation of our vital instincts and sensuous impulses into a living experience. It is recognition of the transcendent reality beyond all particularity. Beauty incorporates our apparatus of apperception and conscious reflection, our capacity to reason beyond finite possibilities, and our ongoing process of coming to self-awareness into a concept of universality.

Beauty is not an ossified doctrine that proscribes a manner of representation as either beautiful or not. This misconception has been the source of much of the criticism lodged against beauty. Even during periods when artistic ideals held dictatorial powers over artistic production, the notion of what constituted the beautiful was always changing. The beauty of facial scarification is as meaningful to the aboriginal tribe member as were Paul Peter Rubens's (1577–1640) ample-bosomed ladies to the seventeenth-century aristocracy. Those who rebelled against beauty as a sentimental attachment to the past failed to recognize beauty as a living and transendental experience.

The expression "beauty is in the eyes of the beholder" aptly describes beauty's transcendent nature as both unique and universal. Beauty is the synthesis of our past experiences into a new situation.

SCIENCE

Science formulates its own system of ethics. There are permissible modes of conduct, and science rejects out of hand what its own system cannot accommodate. Science refuses to deal with the inexplicable. As an ideal, science is rational and aspires to a transcendent reality beyond finite possibilities. In no other discipline is the rational axiom as strenuously adhered to.

Yet science as a transcendent idea has progressed along with humankind. Any idea will loose its transcendent quality when it becomes embedded in objectified doctrines and does not call upon the individual to engage in the discoveries of new territories. For science, these new territories are the inexplicable. Therefore it is human transcendence that must force the issue with the "facts." However, only on the rarest occasions did new discoveries completely alter the existing body of scientific knowledge, and then only because of previous misconceptions.

When science asserts itself into the realm of aesthetics it is always at the expense of humanity's subjective contribution. The generally valid doctrines of science are pragmatic; they are not intended as metaphysical expressions of human subjectivity. When artists incorporate scientific innovations into their artwork, such as computer enhanced audio-visuals and kinetic response sculpture, we are not seeing some aspect of our subjectivity manifest as a metaphysical object. We are seeing our subjective self edged out by the objective manifestation of science, an all-too-common occurrence in an age of all-consuming technology.

As the technological order takes over, the spiritual order is banished into the nocturnal regions of occultism and spiritualism. Spiritualists proclaim that technological progress has been at the cost of our spiritual diminishment. They point to the already discernible alienation of humans from each other, and predict devastating consequences for the future of the species. These consequences are already making themselves felt in aesthetics as the art world witnesses the complete breakdown of any aesthetic system in a Bacchanalian atmosphere of "anything goes." The spiritual separation of human beings from each other is seeing a corresponding fragmentation in the realm of aesthetics. The question then becomes: Is spiritual separation our destiny as science and technology advance?

THE TWENTIETH CENTURY

The Industrial Revolution completely changed the configuration of the landscape. Concrete and steel pierced the natural horizon, and factory chimneys spewed their byproduct of progress. As the dawn of the twentieth century approached, technological advancements would affect every field of aesthetic pursuit: painting, sculpture, architecture, literature, and the performing arts.

In 1908, the movement known as futurism came into being. The futurists found ultimate redemption in the progress of technology. They claimed that the significance of their time was embodied in the dynamism and speed of high-powered machinery in action. The Futurist Manifesto describes a high-speed car ride that ends in near disaster as the automobile wrecks outside a factory, only to have the occupant crawl out and become baptized in industrial waste.

The First World War would change many artists' opinions on the virtues of technology and industrial progress: it gave birth to a movement that espoused the futility and potential for disaster that industrialization presented—the Dada Movement. The Dadaists were intent on destroying all existing values. They were antidoctrinarians to the point of being anarchists. The most significant figure to emerge from this movement was Marcel Duchamp (1884–1968). Duchamp claimed that the only value worthy of artistic contemplation was the creative act of the artist. If the artist chose a ready-made toilet bowl (as Duchamp did) as the object of his aesthetic gratification, the choice itself gave birth to its own new values. This was not a true transvaluation in the Nietzscheian sense. (Nietzsche proclaimed "God is dead" on account of a liberal relativization of values, and called for the creation of new mythologies.[1]) Duchamp's motives were betrayed by his belligerent attitude toward traditional aesthetic values. True transvaluation is "beyond good and evil." We could no more strip ourselves of all our preconceived notions concerning objects by looking at a toilet bowl on a pedestal than we could by looking into thin air. The object of our contemplation becomes merely the contextual ripping of the debased object out of its original meaning. The contextual field of meaning does not change. Our perceptions are superficially wrenched out of context, but not sufficiently to overcome our more deeply seated intuitions and instincts. Our response comes in the form of agitation, suspicion, and hostility, and these feelings are communicated to us by the despair of the artist lost in negativity.

The insistence on the primacy of the creative act, whereby human freedom gives birth to its own values, has been the single most important idea to confront art in the twentieth century. The basis of this idea is a concept of truth as formulated by the school of philosophical thought known as *existentialism*. There is truth in any subjective act to the extent that it manifests itself in the world, that any thought reveals its own existence, or as Søren Kierkegaard simply put it: "Truth is subjectivity."

As existential philosophy took root in the years between the world wars; it had a profound effect on artistic production. The subjective truth of the creative act became the justification of every art movement. Surrealism, abstract expressionism, pop art, minimalism, and conceptual art all have their origin in the existential maxim that truth is subjectivity. The progression of these art movements, as embodied in modern aesthetics, represents a chain reaction of diametrically opposed theories, prone as artists are to finding their own justification in repudiating their predecessors. The effect is to produce a multitude of subjective truths that, when communicated through the object, become strictly conditional. Artworks based on theoretical speculations make no unconditional demands on the viewer. They are only taxing on our intellects.

Existentialism's philosophical half brother is the discipline of *phenomenology,* the science of the essences, or sense-giving properties, of phenomenon. The central claims of this science is the existence of a primordial, prereflective, preobjective, antepredicative contextual field of meanings which secondarily establish itself as the text of our reflective thought. Phenomenology insists on the existence of this prereflective field as the prerequisite for our consciousness to have the ability to fill up with content—indeed, this field provides the text.[2] It further establishes the nexus between this prereflective field and objective reality, as the intentional act, or habit, which unites with its object as a result of the constant tension between the field and the act. Phenomenologists use the term "nature" for field, and the term "freedom" for act. Phenomenology defines this relationship as two aspects of one totality. This science also provides for a "phenomenological reduction" whereby essences are "bracketed" out of their situational meanings in order to ascertain the essences "doxic primordial giveness," which ultimately allows us to conjecture on the possibilities of essences beyond experiential objects.

At the bottom of this highly speculative chain of events, which serves to unite all theoretical aspects of the phenomenon to its primordial, prereflective field, are the concepts of intentionality and attention. A common piece of cutlery can provide an illustration. As we shovel food into our mouth with a fork, our intention, and therefore our attention, is on eating. We do not bring to mind the molten igot as it emerged from the fiery furnance to be forged into a fork. Nor are we aware of the iron ore that first had to be mined and smelted. Yet the entire history of the fork is there, in our hand, if only our attentions can be made aware of it.

The intentional act of the artist should enable us to coordinate this prereflective field of information into an object of aesthetic contemplation if the artist is successful in directing our attention to it. As aesthetic guidelines these two concepts are highly unreliable because their appearance in the individual is attributed to psychological predisposition. If an artist's intention is to communicate a particular thought, the viewer's attention must be geared toward that intentional act. If the artist's intention is to posit a value hitherto unrealized prior to the creative act, somehow the viewer's attention must pool from the prereflective field of meaning the intention of the artist. How this is actually done becomes a job for psychology, which claims access to this hidden, subconscious, antepredicative field of meaning, which it labels the collective unconscious. Psychology thus became an important component in the justification of much modern art.

As a result of the slow dissolution of any encompassing idea to which human spiritual needs could cling, and by which our collective spiritual awareness could be pooled together, art no longer afforded an explicit expression of human spiritual accomplishments. But our spiritual needs were not eliminated; they were merely sublimated because of an inadequate means of finding explicit redemption. Unable to control these spiritual conflicts that continued to beg reconciliation, only subconsciously, human beings began to express themselves symbolically through dreams, and through art works. It then became necessary to establish a consistent framework by which these symbolic representations could be given clear and precise meaning. This became the task of psychology.

Psychology and anthropology have been the disciplines responsible for producing an umbrella of constancy concerning the meanings of human symbolic representations throughout history. Through a system of interpretations, and cross references of ancient mythologies, primitive fairy tales, religious incantations, alchemic proscriptions, dreams, and artworks, these disciplines compiled a list of recurring symbols which were called "archetypes." These archetypes were representative of a world of unconscious tendencies that are in opposition to and in constant conflict with, the human conscious ego. The struggle represents our urge toward absolute self-awareness, the union of the conscious and subconscious. The symbol thus conceived is a metaphysical object, a reconciliation of opposites attributable to the dichotomy of human nature.

Psychology itself admits the flaws inherent in this methodology. It is based on inductive reasoning and therefore does not attempt to create a real picture of this psychological struggle in concrete form, but merely uses a variety of experiences within human knowledge and understanding to arrive at general conclusions. The psychoanalyst, armed with a wealth of historical interpretations and clinical diagnoses, is trained to guide people toward a better understanding of an internal conflict that might manifest itself in severe psychological disorders. Whether or not the analyst is successful will be determined by the response of the client. However, when applied to symbolic representations as manifest in works of art, the success of the interpretation becomes practically unverifiable, to the point of turning the artwork into an article of faith. Furthermore, with the preponderance of market considerations in the modern art world, these psychological interpretations of artwork become highly suspect.

A comprehensive survey of art criticism of the last fifty years would reveal that no "constancy" approach has been employed in interpreting symbols in works of art. In fact the opposite is true. While psychology assumes a scientific method and dispells with aberrations that do not conform to the body of existing data, modern art theory has come to prize the newborn value self-generated with the creative act. The problem is then one of bestowing intelligible meaning on the symbolic representation, and because we are here dealing with new experiences and values, even inductive reasoning will be of no avail. The giving of aesthetic meaning to these artworks becomes an act *a posteriori*. If the art critic were a true clairvoyant, we might be able to trust his judgment. But because he is guided by other claims and motives, the strongest of which is self-aggrandizement, we are justified in questioning his verdicts. In truth the modern art critic operates on much the same level as the shaman of primitive societies. While the shaman is concerned with bestowing meaning upon the great unknown beyond the corporeality of existence, the art critic is concerned with bestowing meaning to a vast hitherto unknown body of knowledge called aesthetics. The shaman and the art critic are viewed as being especially adept at their respective vocations because of some psychological predisposition, while in reality they are both directed by the same ulterior motive, namely their careers.

MODERN ARCHITECTURE

The rapid industrialization and growth of technology in the twentieth century has had a profound effect on humankind's spiritual being. As the techneutronic mass order becomes more encroaching in every aspect of life, we begin to lose our sense of identity, and become alienated and withdrawn. This homogenizing effect on human beings is well illustrated by the rise of modern architecture.

Architecture has always been a reflection of the human spirit as well as a material abode. In the first two decades of this century the pragmatic idea that "form follows function" was first applied to workers' housing, and was to affect all architecture for half a century. These first dwellings were small, functional, modular, and identical. New units could be added at random. These living units were also meant to express an attitude of equality among humans, while in fact they condemn workers to a uniform collectivity at the expense of individuality. Human beings lose their identity and are absorbed into the system. The surrender of our self-identity to a collective idea is a surrender of our subjective will. We become objects in the perpetuation of an apparatus, totally dehumanized.

We need only refer to "urban blight" to recognize the manner in which technology takes out its revenge on humanity. This is also demonstrated by what actually evolved out of the ideas first applied to the housing of the lower class. Expanded to a city block, and rising 100 stories, the modular concept gave rise to the city sky-scraper—the consummate symbol of the corporate hierarchy.

NOTES

1. Friedrich Nietzsche, *The Joyful Wisdom* (New York: Russell and Russell, 1964), #24.

2. Edmund Husserl, *General Introduction to Pure Phenomenology* (New York: Collier Books, 1962), chap. 6, p. 155.

3

Freedom and Convention in Art

I

Freedom is an occurrence that objectifies itself in the world as choice; it is the act of choosing among alternatives with the expectation of return. When the act of choosing is among objective relativities, what is gained is something measurable, a simple preponderance of this over that. When the act of choosing is based on the individual's subjective motives in the form of either compliance or noncompliance to a substantive norm, what is gained is the immeasurability of self-becoming, immeasurable because it is always en route. In the first case, the act is conditional upon arrival at the relative alternative. In the latter, the choice is unconditional in that the object of our choice is the transcendent selves with which we are always at a distance.

Freedom is in constant peril from the restrictions imposed by authority. The danger lies in an authority that tends to become objective and absolute in itself. Whether the result of the powerful will of a leader or a rationally determined dialectic, the authority that aspires to be an absolute end will view all activity, even the subjective acts of individuals, as being directed toward the perpetuation of that end. Subjective beings are turned into objects at the cost of their unconditional freedom. What results is a stagnant collectivity where the human transcendent self becomes subservient to the collectivity. In this situation any free choice is strictly conditional.

Unconditional choice requires the active participation and decision of the individual. The decision, in its most primary form, is either compliance or noncompliance, and the decision is determined by the subject's motives and claims with the aim of achieving an end. Because the object of unconditional choice is the self that the individual is always in the process of becoming, the means of unconditional choice is always directed toward further means of self-becoming. Conditional acts are always arrived at with the conditional choice as object. An unconditional act never reaches its object but it is always directed toward the transcendent selves that the subject projects into the future.

Unconditional freedom is engendered by compliance or non-compliance with a substantive norm against which our decisions are determined—in other words, an authority. There is no unconditional choice without an authority by which we decide either to comply or not to comply. If we choose not to comply, we must suffer the consequences. When the subjective act of the individual is in non-compliance with an authority, unconditionality is achieved in exile or revolt. Compliance with an authority can achieve unconditionality when the absolute authority is also given ethical authority, when through the subjective acts individuals see in compliance the redemption of their future selves in an ethical community. It is a giving of themselves in return for security. Both conditional and unconditional freedom require the presence of authority: in the first instance, for the objective ends and alternatives, in the latter, as the resistence against which we project our future selves in becoming. Without authority there is no freedom, conditional or otherwise—only anarchy.

II

Conventions of representations in art have developed at different times and at different places. Conventions are established by way of custom and usage, and a society's sociopolitical and geographic characteristics will determine the strength and staying power of its conventions. In periods of long-term stability, conventions have endured for centuries, becoming ossified and stagnant. At times of rapid change, conventions can barely be established before being swept away by the tide of history. Or a convention may go through a process of superficial embellishment, becoming a parody of its former self.

Conventions were initially established to give comprehensibility to our metaphysical needs. When primitive men shaped their fetishes and idols, they had to be sure their meaning was understood. The convention provided the common language. This function of the convention developed colaterally with our attempts to bridge the abyss that seemed to separate our own spirit with the great world spirit. The convention became part and parcel with our establishment in the rational drive toward an ethical community. The convention provided concrete and tangible manifestations to something human-kind felt in its soul, intangible and inexplicable. That which is in-explicable among our soulful yearnings take shape as a metaphysical object. The art object thus provides, by means of convention, its own metaphysical component. Convention provides the art object with a comprehensible means to express transcendence.

Cycladic art provides an early example of a convention employed by human metaphysical needs. Minoan civilization flourished from 3200 B.C.E. in the Aegean Islands known as the Cyclades. Cycladic figurines from around 3000 B.C.E. display a remarkable similarity. Monolithic and schematic, they are almost invariably female, with shield-like faces, triangular noses, small breasts, and arms folded across the abdomen. The exact purpose of these figurines is unknown but they were in all likelihood cult figures associated with the hereafter. The enigmatic and streamlined timelessness of these figures could have been created in a futuristic world. There is an eternal power in these figures. These idols were produced for many hundreds of years, until the Cyclades were invaded by the mainland around 1500 B.C.E. Two thousand years later, primitive people on Easter Island, completely isolated and unaware of their Cycladic predecessors, would again conventionalize the human figure into monolithic, angular, and schematic statues.

Similarities in the development of these metaphysical conventions is well documented in the circular mandala with its radiating "qua-ternio." The circular mandala is symbolic of complete self-awareness, a union of the body and spirit, of the conscious and unconscious. This idea of a transcendental totality of the self must synthesize the metaphysical polarities of existence into a unity. This is represented by the four regions of the quaternio—humankind's unique character as appearing in time is united with the universal and eternal. If humans have a spiritual and good side, there lurks in the "shadow" the material and evil side, expressed in Christian theology as the anti-christ. These expressions of humans coming to complete self-awareness are motivated by our rational drive to an encompassing totality. In Egyptian mythology it is depicted by the god Horus and his four sons. In Christian interpretation it finds expression in Christ and the four evangelists. The mandala and quaternio is a common occurrence in the art of the Pueblo and Navajo Indians of the American Southwest, and the most exquisite examples are to be found among the Buddhists of Tibet.

III

Realism, or fidelity to nature, cannot be considered a convention as such. All perception of any particular appearance is always conditioned by the integral abstract configurations that lie beneath the ephemeral exterior. There is no better illustration of this dichotomy than that found in the classical ideal as presented in the sculpture of ancient Greece. The ideality, balance, and symmetry of the perfect human figure was based on geometric abstraction, calculated with the precision of a mathematical formula.

While representation itself is not a convention, the manner in which objects and ideas are represented has been conventionalized time and again. This conventionalization occurred primarily in two forms. First, as new materials and techniques were discovered, there evolved a conventional approach in utilizing the materials to render an appearance. In painting these practices included modeling with light and shade, a unified single point perspective, balance of composition by use of point and counterpoint, foreshortening of objects in space, and painting in layers to attain transparencies in depth and variegated textures. These means of representing appearances had first to be discovered, generally accepted, adopted, and thus conventionalized. The second area of conventionalization was in the development of a system of signs and symbols. The mandala is an archetype symbol of total self-awareness. Christian iconography is replete with symbolic significance: for example, the miraculous conception as the symbol for the birth of spiritual love, a birth completely independent of corporeality. Much secular painting of the sixteenth and seventeenth centuries also adhered to a strict format of symbolic imagery; a peacock was symbolic of virility, a poplar was symbolic of stability and endurance, and a dog at his master's feet was symbolic of loyalty.

The convention or the manner in which appearances are technically rendered, and the convention of symbolic representation, have each played a significant part in the overall progress of art. With technique, artists have always been proud of their native skills, abilities, and facilities, and the greatest practitioners of their craft have always been considered the greatest contributors to the convention of their art. Titian, Velazquez, Rembrandt, Hals, Courbet, Manet, and Cezanne were all pioneers of their craft whose contributions were later absorbed into the stock-in-trade of convention. Symbolic conventions have also taken art into new places. Today artists work with a diverse array of particularly modern symbols. The pop artists of the 1960s chose "popular" imagery of soup cans, flags, comic books, and the like to convey the idea that ordinary objects could be used in such a way as to say as much about the human condition, and about painting, as if these objects were rendered in the conventional "picture" manner. This development was a knee-jerk reaction to the previous convention—that of abstraction—which held that subject content in a painting was a sentimental distraction from the painting's formal elements and psychological impact.

IV

While art was still in the service of religion and the state, convention was strictly adhered to. Art was an expression of the ideals embodied in the nation. The means of depicting these ideals were specific and beyond question. The artist was not free to express personal feelings, and the idea of an original conception was alien to the artist's thinking. Developments in the fifteenth century would completely change this relationship of the artist to his work and would eventually allow the personality of the artist to assert itself. But this development of the unique personality of the artist did not represent any democratic or egalitarian reform. Art remained intolerant of any form of rebellion against convention.

In 1527, Rome was sacked by the forces of Emperor Charles V thus bringing to an end the cultural developments of the Renaissance. The ironclad conventions of the classical Renaissance had been established during the first quarter of the sixteenth century. Structural balance of composition, harmonious gradations of atmospheric qualities, ideal representation of the human form, and a polished picture surface, were all central to the Renaissance aesthetic. The collapse of the ethical institutions of religion and the state removed the restrictions formally imposed by those institutions. Aesthetics was no longer determined by ethical expression; it now had to find its own means of locomotion. Convention thus became the authority by which aesthetics found its motivation to change. All future developments in aesthetics would be in the form of either compliance or noncompliance to the current convention.

Michelangelo was the first to impose his resistance against the classical convention, a convention he helped to create. His figural distortions in the spandrels of the Sistine Chapel (1512) were a kinetic release of what had been a powerful reserve trapped within the classic ideal. Paintings were no longer constructed with symmetrical balance. Asymmetrical compositions were designed with dramatic directional emphasis. Ideal representation of the human form gave way to an elongated and expressive rendition as employed by the mannerists. These rebellions against convention by Titian, Correggio, and Tintoretto, would transform the classical convention into the baroque convention.

Baroque aesthetics remained in vogue for over two centuries. Its conventions were malleable enough to allow great talents to assert themselves, as well as lesser artists to produce credible if uninspired paintings. Counted among the former group would be Rubens, Claude Lorraine, Velazquez, Vermeer, Guardi, Watteau, and Chardin. The greatest master of this period was unquestionably Rembrandt (1609–1669). Rembrandt brought to his paintings an enhanced sensitivity of observation, a superiority in the handling of the painting material, and a penetrating psychological insight to his subject matter. No one factor can be attributed to the greatness of Rembrandt, who was the eleventh child of a country miller. Certainly the power of his personality cannot be denied. It can also be confidently stated that it was within the convention of his day that this great genius made the most magnificent contributions to the art of painting.

By the middle of the eighteenth century, baroque aesthetics had reached an impasse. The Enlightenment had created a new interest in the balance and clarity of classicism. New historical discoveries and treatises on antiquity, particularly those of Winckelmann and Gibbon, fired the imagination of such artists as Antonio Canova

(1751–1822) and Jacques-Louis David, the two artists most closely identified with the neoclassicism of the late eighteenth century. For the most part the neoclassicists indulged in an overidealized conception that rendered their paintings fatuous. The notable exception is Jean Auguste Ingres (1780–1867), whose manipulation of ideal anatomy and tonal gradations imparted a contemplative austerity to the classic ideal.

Neoclassicism was short-lived. As a product of the Enlightenment, it was supposed to bring painting back to a rationally valid ideal. The French Revolution, the Reign of Terror, and the horrors of the Napoleonic Wars would bring human reason into question, and bring into focus the madness behind rational speculations. Goya, perhaps by his own despondent disposition, was to vividly grasp this truth of his age. His paintings display the hypocrisy of his times with a complete fidelity to the truth as he saw it with his own eyes. Goya reflects a new rebellion against rationalizations and unattainable absolutes. His was an art that would point to a new expression of personal emotions as embodied by the romantic movement.

The aesthetic pendulum, first making bold advances into new territories upon the steed of emotionalism, then making steady retreats into the domain of formalized principles, held the polarities of this dichotomy within the same precincts. Classicists and romanticists still conceived of their paintings according to certain conventions and their ideas were then constructed into paintings in the studio. A radically new approach to painting would soon take the artist out of the studio and into the fresh air.

The impressionists were the first to reject the convention of their day with the confidence that they had arrived at a new manner of representation of greater compelling certainty. They discarded the earthy umbers and dark bituminous palette of the academies and substituted opaque and pastel hues. They excluded objects solidly colored and concentrated on the diffusion of light as the operative of color and form. If the impressionists held on to anything from the past it was the basic rudiments of atmospheric perspective—that objects and colors are more defined in the foreground, and diffuse and obscure in the background. It would be Cezanne who would grab hold of these last vestiges of convention and completely reshape them. With Cezanne we see an equalized color scheme; objects in the background are seen with the same intensity as in the foreground.

With Cezanne a consistent perspective or viewpoint dissolves into the relationships between planes. These were the most radical departures from convention ever witnessed at that time. The cubists of the first decade of the twentieth century would pick up where Cezanne left off, turning his equalized color scheme into a system of complete recessional flatness. This practice became quickly adopted and conventionalized throughout Europe.

V

The greatest accomplishments in art have been achieved while the influence of convention was the strongest. When the art object makes tangible human metaphysical needs, the communicative fulfillment is provided by the convention. Greatness in art must be accompanied by some form of measurability. Convention provides the means for such calculation through its communicability. If art has progressed it must have done so in relation to where it has been. Progress implies a continuum to which new artistic ideas are linked. The genius of Michelangelo was nurtured and brought forth by the strict control imposed by the rigid conventionality of the classical ideal as formulated in the Renaissance. The great power of Rembrandt could not have found expression if a devitalized convention had not offered the opportunity to surpass it.

If we look at a convention as a set of rules and laws to guide us, we might conclude that the convention subjects artistic production to a limitation, when in fact the convention provides a natural field of resistance the boundaries of which could be pushed onward into hitherto unknown territories. For the sake of illustration, let us say that over a period of time a convention has evolved based upon the construction of a four-inch square. All artistic production must find its origin and foundation on the four-inch square. They might be arranged lengthwise, diagonally, intersecting, or all askew—two inches apart, or maybe two feet. They may be blue, black, orange, or tutti-frutti. Four four-inch squares could be arranged in such a fashion that they produce an eight-inch square, with perhaps a dotted line to indicate the original four-inch squares. In time this dotted line might disappear, becoming common knowledge that the eight-inch square was indeed four squares of four inches. By establishing our convention on the four-inch square, we have created the potential of infinite variation. These variations on the four-inch square may have existed theoretically before the convention was ever established, but by establishing the convention the resistence was created against which the choice was made to bring that variety into the world. However, no one would fail to recognize the strict conditionality of our convention.

The idea that the conventional is something marked by "ordinariness" because it adheres to established norms, is a misunderstanding of the liberating effect the convention can have on the individual who is seeking real self-affirmation. It is to confuse the conventional with the academic. All academic works are conventional. When the artist takes the convention as an end in itself his artistic production will take a perfunctory approach in compliance with the convention. The artist has surrendered some freedom. It is a lack of courage to assert oneself in exchange for the security of being a participant in the norm. Finding a peaceable home in a codified system, the artwork will be academic and lack distinction.

If the artist views the convention solely as a means, as a point of departure, and if his native capacities are of the right mixture of temperment, skill, and determination, he may lift the parameters of convention to new heights. The conventional is no longer academic. If the talent of the artist is of such a magnitude as to add to the convention's greatest measure, he has transformed the convention in his own image. His self-affirmation has found an objective home. By becoming the convention itself he has achieved a form of immortality. By perfecting convention he has both accepted and rejected convention, uniting the poles of opposites that seek transcendental fulfillment.

By the same token the artist who completely rejects convention out of hand risks complete surrender of his unconditional freedom. The artist may have any number of justifications for this decision but, for whatever reason, he must replace the transcendent source of his self-affirmation, otherwise he is simply lost in negation or has attempted to make absolute and perfectable some isolated body of knowledge. In the first case, the artist, unable to manage his situation becomes lost in despair. In the second, his choice is conditional upon the objective relativities. Both cases abnegate unconditional self-affirmation.

CONCLUDING REMARKS

Art is a living experience with transcendental qualities, an existential experience of infinite variety based on each individual's historically determined subjectivity. This experience lives in communication, and only through communication can art fulfill its metaphysical duty by bringing each of us into a state of greater self-awareness in the form of our transcendental self. In that each one of us is different historically and subjectively, art must be an experience both unconditional and universal.

The communicative act that results in an experience of art is the transmission of an idea from artist to art object to viewer. The communication does not take place with the object, but by means of the object. The metaphysical object remains as a cipher of the transcendental universality of the idea that the artist is trying to convey. The object itself does not transcend. Transcendence is the being of that part of existence that lacks all objectivity—the actual process of becoming in existence. Once objectified it is no longer transcendence; however, the comprehensible communicability of the idea can be looked upon as the object's "transcendental residue."

All ideas influence our lives, even if that influence is negative or indifferent. Some ideas, like liberty, justice, and love, make their presence felt more explicitly in our lives. Other ideas seem to occupy more specialized areas of concern, like the ramifications of a scientific method, the semantics of word definitions, and the psychology of social relations. It is apparent that some ideas are central to the lives of all human beings while others only occupy the periphery of our attentions. Whether an idea is central or peripheral depends upon the magnitude of the transcendental residue.

Why do some ideas communicate to us more directly than others? The answer resides in the magnitude of the metaphysical need that calls upon the idea for objective fulfillment. A majority of people desire to live in a peaceful, ethical community, whether it be secular or religious in nature. By virtue of the base transcendental contribution of all people desiring a better tomorrow in an ethical community, an art object communicating these ethical ideas will provide a greater metaphysical function by means of its greater transcendental residue. Metaphysics is thus the mechanism by which we are meant to have tangible access to transcendence.

When art no longer serves as the vehicle for communicating an ethical value, the object must still be provided a substantive norm if it is to engender unconditional self-awareness. As the metaphysical need to find spiritual communion with our fellow human beings recedes into a highly material conception of humanity, and humankind encloses itself within its personal idea of spiritual redemption based on appropriation and wealth, spiritual dissolution is manifest.

What is to replace the transcendental source of our unconditional self-fulfillment in the face of ethical disenfranchisement? It can only be replaced by an authority against which we can risk unconditional freedom. People can achieve unconditionality in compliance with authority because that compliance admits consent, and consent invests authority with ethical justification. All then becomes a question of fidelity representing the extent to which an individual is loyal to the transcendental source of his self-affirmation. The human betrayal of self-affirmation in compliance with authority represents an act of "bad faith."[1] We surrender all freedom and become an object in a meaningless situation beyond our control.

Lack of fidelity to any life conception other than material contentment leads to spiritual separation. This is evident in contemporary artworks. Modern art parades an endless succession of incommunicable images of despair crying in the night. These are true reflections of our dehumanized spiritual separation, and as such they deserve to stand as testaments of our time, a time when it is simply more profitable, and therefore desirable, "to err with a genius than hit the mark with the crowd."[2]

NOTES

1. Jean-Paul Sartre, *Being and Nothingness* (New York: Washington Square Press, 1966), p. 86.
2. Miguel de Unamuno, *Tragic Sense of Life* (New York: Dover, 1954).

Part Two

VALUES

4

$$$ and Aesthetics

I

Art and money have been likened to each other in a confused way. The system by which value is assigned to money is completely alien and in many ways antagonistic to that by which values are assigned in the realm of aesthetics. Yet behind the high dollar value paid for a work of art there is the veiled implication of a corresponding high aesthetic value. The manner by which material values and aesthetic values are established are irreconcilable and defy integration. The justifications for the price of a work of art are nonaesthetic.

Art exists within the realm of aesthetics, money exists within that of economics: the latter evolved out of considerations that were materialistic, while aesthetics are more spiritual in nature. Materialism deals with things that are concrete, spiritualism with the more abstract. The abstract takes form in the realm of ideas; objects are concrete. This series of comparisons is mutually antagonistic. Some of them, like the material and spiritual, or the concrete and abstract, are metaphysical opposites—their definitions are determined by contradicting the other. It is not surprising, then, that so many view the metaphysical definition of human as comprised of body and soul.

If there is something that comes close to being a true conciliation of these two opposing spheres, it would be the art object. Art gives to an abstract idea the form of a concrete object. The object is the

This chapter is an expanded and adapted version of "Dollars and Aesthetics," *Chronicles* (March 1993).

vehicle for the idea; it is what makes the idea tangible. Art is the communication of ideas.

There are many artful ideas that lack concrete objects; a piece of music is one example. The idea being communicated through music does not have a concrete manifestation as does a painting or a sculpture. There are objects of thought that remain intangible. Freedom is an idea that manifests itself in an occurrence that involves choice. Compassion describes a situation where by means of identification one human being enters into a spiritual communion with another. And prior to taking form as an object of thought, all ideas exist in a formless intuitive state.

Money occupies a comparative relation to that of art. There is a signification to money beyond the mere corporeal presence of the paper or coin on which the denomination is printed or stamped. Money stands as a record and reserve of the practicality of our efforts waiting to be redeemed in objects of our desire.

There is a major obstacle obstructing the bridge between the realm of material and aesthetic values. Material values are arrived at via motivations that are hedonistic and practical. We place a value on those things that give us pleasure, and we find to have value those things that work. Aesthetic values are arrived at due to peoples' ethical and moral motivations, the felt urge to enter into communication, to seek out those things we share in common, our need to coexist in harmony.

Value is the worth of a thing, however that worth is translated: money, goods, sentiment, etc. Value is that quality of a thing that makes it more or less desirable. A value is a belief or standard. But these are only definitions of value; they do not explain how values are developed. Values are arrived at as the result of an action motivated by a subjective affectivity. We are affected by desires because there is something lacking in our lives. We take action to acquire those things that we lack, and when we acquire them our desires are satisfied, and that we find to be of value. The action we take to satisfy our desires, when viewed as a whole, is the work we perform during the course of our lives. By working we are rewarded for our efforts with money. Money represents a record and reserve of our efforts. We work in order to accumulate money to buy those things that bring us pleasure.

The effort that each individual expends is itself assigned a different value. Intellectual efforts are highly regarded, yet teachers, researchers, and scholars are not highly rewarded for their efforts. Manual laborers receive less than those with learned skills. Professional athletes are highly rewarded for their ability. And why do corporate executives receive high salaries? Because they have been successful in providing a good or service that a sufficient number of people consider desirable, possessing enough "value," and on which these people are willing to expend their efforts and money. Our materialistic values are hedonistic and practical. We place value on things that bring us pleasure, and things that work.

Can the manner by which aesthetic values are established be adequately explained? If art is the communication of ideas, is there a way to measure the magnitude of the communication and assign to it a comparative value? All communication involves a process, an occurrence or transmission. The artist is the transmitter, the viewer is the receiver, and the art object is the beacon or relay station by which the idea is transmitted. If the viewer understands and appreciates the idea that the artist is trying to convey, that viewer has found the work aesthetically gratifying. Aesthetic gratification is different from material satisfaction. Gratification is extended or offered in return for a gift or favor.

Aesthetic gratification is the process of identification one has, with the idea being conveyed by the work of art. Art tells us something about ourselves or about our world that, deep down inside, we already know. This process of identification reverts to the pre-objective, formless intuitive state of the idea being communicated. All aesthetic activity begins at this intuitive level.

Intuition is a feeling of certainty about reality based on the two irreducible contingencies of existence that are our access to the nature of things: space, into which we have access by means of our bodies, and time, into which we have access by means of our consciousness, or that part of our substance that thinks—what some call the soul. That is how the art object unites object and idea, and why the art object constitutes a true metaphysical reconciliation. Our intuitions are aided by impressions of a sensory nature—sights, sounds, and feelings—which find outlet in the imagination as the expressive production of an art form.

The process of identification that engenders aesthetic gratification is a testament to the intuitive foundation that all thinking beings share. This quality of sharing is what intimately links aesthetics with ethics. Our aesthetic value system is a direct reflection of our moral fiber and our ethical priorities; the greatest artistic productions have always been created as an attempt to convey some ethical message.

An objection may be raised at this point: Have there not been supreme aesthetic acheivements that have made no attempt to convey an ethical message? What of a still life by Chardin, or a landscape by Van Gogh, or a self-portrait by Rembrandt? All of these carry an implicit message of the community of all people. Artists are giving us a new way of looking at our world. They are sharing an intuition they have had, but we all have in common. That is the most important issue addressed by ethics: striving to find what human beings have in common that will enable them to live together in harmony. A self-portrait by Rembrandt, in which the artist bares his soul and speaks to us by saying, "look at me, I am a man with all the weaknesses and foibles that a man is capable of," instills far more identification with, and compassion for, our fellow humans than a religious painting depicting angels and miracles.

The world of finance and the world of aesthetics engage in transactions, though the financial transaction is far more easily understood. There is a tradeoff, an exchange. First, our efforts are traded into something that is meant to stand in its stead to be redeemed later for objects of our desire. Too often, we come to rely on material redemption to bring about our spiritual redemption; obtaining the objects of our desire becomes the source of our happiness.

The financial transaction and the aesthetic transaction are completely independent. When painters sell paintings to support themselves, they are engaged in a financial transaction. Such transactions are consummated in material redemption and are thus turned into acts of appropriation. This is the essence of what has long been called the Protestant work ethic. We work in order to have and make the world ours. "Doing" and "having" are the fundamental existential building blocks in "becoming."[1]

The aesthetic transaction, on the other hand, is the communication of an idea, and its consummation is a spiritual communion. The aesthetic commodity is the idea that gives reason for believing in the unity of all human beings. The process of identification aspires to union in the ethical community. Aesthetic transactions aspire to spiritual redemption; they are acts of sharing. The aesthetic transaction also aspires to metaphysical redemption, making a whole of the polarities of giving and taking. People who only take cannot be spiritually whole; they must also give to complete the cycle. Gratitude is the residual of sharing.

Taken to its ultimate conclusion, the fundamental aesthetic commodity is love, god's love. Not the God who sits in judgment, for that is a vindictive God. Not the God whose eminent perfection is the final cause, for that is a guilt-ridden God. But the god that is the greatest idea man can have of himself: unconditional love for one's fellow beings. This is a commodity that cannot be bought or sold; it defies justification within the matrix of materialism. This is why aesthetic values and material values can never be adequately reconciled.

II

There has been a fundamental change in the nature of art since the dawn of civilization: it has shifted from the spiritual to the material. The art of the primitives, of the ancients, and of medievals, was much more spiritual than that of modern artists. The older traditions appealed to a higher power, or advocated some ethical communion, including the glorification of a powerful ruler. During the Renaissance this fundamental change started to take shape. Art first became wed to science, particularly through the agencies of perspective and anatomy. Organized ethical authority was diminished by virtue of its own corrupt practices. Aesthetics no longer found itself dictated by the source of the ethical message. The manner of conveying ideas was now guided and fostered by the spirit of investigation born in the Renaissance. The principal players in this shift were Michelangelo and Titian. Their work represented a kinetic release of a powerful reserve trapped within the classical ideal. This marked the beginning of "art for art's sake." Aesthetics was no longer represented by a unified manner of expression, but began to fragment in every direction. This was a conflicting development for aesthetics. It introduced freedom of choice into the matrix of artistic production, and established sophistry of every description as aesthetic authority, while at the same time obfucating the ethical message.

Prior to the Renaissance, artists were viewed more as craftspeople, many of whom were highly paid for their services and honored as celebrities for ably conveying messages as they were instructed. Originality was not considered of particular value and was tolerated only to the extent that it strengthened the ethical message. It was the craftsmen's services that were considered of value. They were commissioned to produce works of art that were didactic in purpose and whose value was determined by the extent to which it acheived this purpose. Artists did not commit to and then produce a work for sale. It is only after the Renaissance, when aesthetics assumed an autonomous function, that the art object was believed to have an intrinsic dollar value. Differing aesthetic theories began to vie for acceptance and preeminence: aesthetic rivalries developed, and fashion came to dictate popular taste.

After the Renaissance, artists first had to contend with either being in or out of fashion. "Style" and "fashion" have for some time been mistakenly identified with one another. It is often said that a painter has gone out of style. What is meant is that a painter's style has gone out of fashion. Style is an aesthetic determination. It is a supra-personal manner of expression that categorizes a period or type of production. Fashion is nonaesthetic, determined by market-ability, promotion, and hype. Fashion caters to the snob—those who don't have the patience, desire, or intelligence to attain the type of education that would allow them to make a comparative aesthetic judgment for themselves. Snobs will, instead, supplant this lack of internal fortitude with a superficial floss that appeals to their sense of self-importance. Because of the snobs' lack of artistic integrity, fashion must necessarily appeal to their vanity. It was Oscar Wilde who defined the cynic as one who knows the price of everything and the value of nothing. This is also the definition of the snob, who, in the final analysis, determines value by price.

Fashion has treated artists of great talent with complete indifference. In his youth, Rembrandt (1606–1669) enjoyed a fashionable period and was awarded important commissions. Later in life, he fell from fashion, yet it is his later work that is considered his best. The Dutch painter Frans Hals (1580?–1666) fared no better: though he was the greatest portrait painter of his time, he died in the poorhouse. Yet Paul Potter (1625–1654), the corny Dutch chronicler of bovine subject matter, was one of the most fashionable painters of seventeenth-century Holland.

In baroque Italy, painters of the first order, such as Antonio Correggio (1494–1534) and Agostino Carracci (1557–1602), lived lives of trial and hardship. Germany was particularly indifferent to its geniuses. The painter Mathias Grunewald (1480?–1530) was hounded all over Germany for his political views before dying penniless, and Casper David Friedrich (1774–1840), perhaps the greatest romantic painter of all, lived his life in abject poverty. The list of great painters whose talents were overlooked—the Van Goghs and Guardis—could be expanded ad infinitum, as could the names of fashionable hacks—the Pradiers and Von Stucks—whose work has drifted into obscurity.

Needless to say, not all geniuses suffered the fate of neglect. Raphael and Rubens lived like princes. Valesquez and Holbein were awarded royal commissions and rewarded admirably for their efforts. However, for every Rubens there is a Hercules Seghers (1590–c. 1638), the first true innovator of landscape, who was so poor that he had to paint on the seat of his worn out trousers. For every Raphael there is a master the rank of Paolo Ucello (1397–1475), who at the age of seventy-two wrote, "I am old and without means of livelihood. My wife is ill, and I can no longer work." These inconsistencies serve to emphasize the arbitrary and fickle nature of recognition in the art world.

III

The American free enterprise system is susceptible to all manner of exploitation and abuse. Bribery, kickbacks, and fraud all seem to be endemic to high finance and particularly to market economies. When government officials are caught taking bribes, they are brought to justice. When corporate leaders are caught making millions by trading insider information, they are thrown in jail. However, the boundary of propriety, and what constitutes legitimate quality of product and service in the art world is not only less discernible, but ambiguous and completely unregulated. In the business of art it is easy to act in a manner completely dishonest, unethical, and immoral, and never do anything illegal.

Substance in the art world is all a matter of illusion and facade. In the words of a maxim of La Rochefoucauld, "To establish oneself in the world one does all one can to seem established there already."[2]

This illusion goes far beyond spending money on fancy advertising and lavish exhibitions to create the appearance of popularity and worth. It entails the manufacturing of artificially high prices for artists' work on the open market. This is achieved through an unspoken collusion between art dealers and auctioneers that involves bribery and price-fixing. Bribes are cloaked by the guise of commissions, and prices are fixed on the auction floor by several randomly placed "ringers" who bid the work up to a predetermined level. Once this is accomplished dealers have a public record with which they can assure their buyers of the safety and investment potential of their artists.

Investment potential and fashion merge in an unholy communion. The investment potential of a work of art, in conjunction with the impetus it receives from invested interests, will determine the rate of appreciation of that work of art. Here is where fashion and market considerations come to dictate taste. An illustration, with the benefit of hindsight, will clarify this point.

The year is 1950 and you have five hundred dollars to spend on a work of art. You could take a walk along tenth street in New York City, wander through the studios of an emerging group of abstract painters, and take home a large oil painting. Or, you could walk into a Madison Avenue gallery that specialized in painters of the nineteenth century and take home a fine example by an American impressionist. Or, you could cross Madison Avenue to an antique shop and buy an exquisite example of sculpture from the Roman Republic.

Now the year is 1990 and you wish to sell the artwork that has been in your possession for the past forty years. You take it to one of the auction houses to have it appraised. If the downtown studio you happened to have visited was Willem de Kooning's (1904-) or Mark Rothko's (1903-1970), you are told that you own a painting worth about one million dollars. If the American impressionist you bought was a well-respected name, like Frederick Frieseke (1874-1939) or Robert Reid (1862-1929), your painting could be worth one hundred thousand dollars. And if you bought an exceptionally fine antiquity that the experts can determine came from a specific location, your sculpture might be worth ten thousand dollars. What accounts for these significant differences in appreciation?

In 1950, abstract expressionists were still the rebel outsiders. It was only during the decade of the 1950s that they truly came into prominence. The price of their work was at ground level, therefore they offered the greatest potential for appreciation. The aesthetic justifications for the skyrocketing prices of these paintings would entail lengthy discourses on philosophy, psychology, sociology, history, even anthropology and other subjects. At bottom is the existential notion that the creative act is value generating, a notion that is a premature qualification of subjectivity. Values are arrived at not by the mere appearance of subjective affectivities, but only after the satisfaction of subjective affectivities. According to Gabriel Marcel in his *The Decline of Wisdom,* "When human freedom claims to give birth to its own values, anarchy takes the place of reason."[3] All philosophical justifications notwithstanding, the work of the abstract expressionists would never have appreciated the way it did if the investment potential had not been there and if these painters had not come under the wing of a very influential group of people, with a lot of money, who, by virtue of their wealth, were able to manipulate the art market, the media, and the promotional apparatus. This group possessed the vanity to believe that they were the architects of culture.

The situation with the American impressionists was different. Many of these painters were successful during their lifetimes, particularly between the years of 1890 and 1910. Most of them made the obligatory trip to Paris to see the work of the innovators of the style, and when they returned to America, they were generally looked upon as provincial counterparts to the Europeans. During the first half of the twentieth century, while the works and reputations of the European impressionists and post-impressionists were rising, the work of the American impressionists was ascending into the storage attics. However, after the World War II, New York City became the capital of the art world. There was renewed emphasis on America and things American, and the American impressionists were rediscovered. Many were recognized for having brought to impressionism a fresh and novel approach. A few have even rivaled the Europeans in market value. The achievements or failures of impressionism notwithstanding, the prices of these paintings would never have escalated had the investment potential not been recognized by dealers and collectors, and had these paintings not been available in abundance for speculation.

The antiques occupy a completely different position. There was no upheaval as in the first two examples. Roman antiquities had reached a level of acknowledgment that didn't falter. They were not at the forefront of what was current, nor did they have the opportunity to be rediscovered. Since antiques were subject to less impetus by invested interests who were after works with the greatest potential for appreciation, their market value increased at a far slower pace.

It must be noted that these illustrations were not designed to judge the aesthetic value of the three works in question. Considered strictly within the context of a financial transaction, these artworks can be looked upon as market commodities, and the illustration was designed to treat the subject as a stock analyst would. The financial transaction and the aesthetic transaction are completely independent, and to "broker" the aesthetic transaction would entail a thorough empirical analysis of the magnitude of the aesthetic communication. On a personal level, aesthetic significance is in large part determined by the demands the individual places on a work of art. The demand that individuals place on a work of art is largely determined by the level of aesthetic understanding they have attained by means of a comprehensive education. By the same token, a work of art invested with aesthetic significance will demand the viewer have that education in order to understand it.

IV

The 1990s have been labeled the techneutronic computer age of information. Everything is at our command at the touch of our fingertips. We want our information fast, and we want to be able to comprehend it fast. The result of this development is a congenital laziness and impatience with things that take time, research, and education. We are becoming a computer literate society, but we are losing many of our other abilities in the bargain. One of these is the ability to make an intelligent value judgment about art. As our ability to communicate aesthetically with other people dissolves, a more insidious development takes place—we become spiritually separated from each other.

A curious paradox says that it is easy to have patience with things that take none. It takes no patience to understand the dollar value of art. It is simple, cold, calculable; it even provides a numerical scale. True aesthetic value takes a great deal of patience to understand. It is unfortunate, but not surprising, that dollar value has come to represent aesthetic value in today's age of impatience.

There is a correlation between artistic understanding and the aesthetic merit of the work of art purchased. While it is possible to convince or cajole a person of meager artistic understanding to buy a work of high artistic merit, in general, they do not want to be confronted with anything that makes any kind of demand on their intelligence. It puts them in the position of becoming aware of their ignorance, which produces a hostile reaction. You will never see a person with a high level of artistic understanding purchase a work of art of low artistic merit.

In addition, it is in general easier to sell artwork of low artistic merit to people of low artistic intelligence. The person of low artistic intelligence doesn't want to make the effort to meet the work of art half way in the communicative process. Aesthetically inferior art fits the bill because the communicative message is nonexistent. It makes no demand on the viewer's understanding. It is for this reason that most of the successful artists of the past half century have lacked true aesthetic significance.

The art market is now experiencing a terrible slump after the impressive gains in the 1980s. This is only in part due to the condition of the economy. It is true that in a sour economy luxury items are the first to be cut from discretionary spending. But the root of the problem lies elsewhere.

The dealers are responsible for pumping up the art market beyond the level that the real situation could maintain. The auction houses are particularly guilty of this. As long as paintings continued to sell they saw no reason to stop the escalation. They steadily raised estimates on paintings, placed high reserves on paintings below which they were not allowed to sell, and started the bidding at high levels. They created an inflated situation in which auctions would contain dozens of paintings estimated at over a million dollars. There simply wasn't enough money to buy all of them. They were priced out of the market and many went unsold. People who had paid good money just a few years ago now could not liquidate their "investment." This sent shock waves through the art market that shook people's confidence in buying art in general.

The critics are also culpable for their part in creating a helter-skelter, "anything goes" aesthetic environment. There is no longer any unified body of aesthetic knowledge to which values can be assigned. If everything and anything can qualify as a work of art, then art loses any sense of definition. Critics are all busy cultivating their own aesthetic orchards, and no one dares trespass to pluck their neighbor's fruit. This fragmentation of aesthetics left no foundation to justify dollar values on the art market, permitting the dealers the opportunity to promote anything without discretion. The highly esoteric and obscure nature of contemporary art criticism offers the enticement of entry into a private and privileged club—this is manna for dealer and snob alike. The magazines that disseminate art criticism are dealers' trade journals whose livelihoods depend on advertising dollars and promoting sales. The critics welcome this scenario; indeed, they look favorably upon works of art attaining astronomical prices. In the absence of any criteria for aesthetic value judgment, these prices are interpreted as confirmations of the critics' aesthetic verdicts.

Ultimately, it is the artists themselves who must assume responsibility for the present state of affairs. They have abnegated their position of propagating the aesthetic message. The decades of the 1950s and 1960s were the age of the critic. The 1970s and 1980s were the decades of the dealer. During these years the "aesthetic ball" was taken away from the artist. Without any sound criteria for value judgment, the artists allowed their aesthetic choices to be made for them and were finally left with no choice of their own. Artists today are working naked in a barren wilderness. They have no means of providing for themselves, and their surroundings offer them no direction and no comfort. This is the symptom of spiritual separation. Artists are groping, hoping to become the next important discovery. Works of art designed to shock the sensibilities are fed into a system that has become anesthetized like an addict in need of a more powerful fix. Like the addict, who, at the center of his discontent, fails to recognize his own problem, so must the art world reach rock bottom before it can come to its own rescue.

NOTES

1. Jean-Paul Sartre, *Being and Nothingness* (New York: Washington Square Press, 1966), p. 557.

2. François de la Rochefoucauld, *The Maxims of La Rochefoucauld* (New York: Random House, 1959), #56.

3. Gabriel Marcel, *The Decline of Wisdom* (New York: Philosophical Library, 1956).

Part Three

TECHNIQUE

5

The Metaphysics of Technique

I

The "technical" is generally associated with technology. So-called technical manuals deal with computer software, engineering, and scientific breakthroughs. When applied to art, the "technical" is considered the handiwork of the commercial artist. Advertising layouts and magazine illustrations are thought of as the products of craftsmen.

The Greek root *techne* originally referred to being skillful in art. This reveals how encompassing art was in the life of Greek society. All facets of life were likened to art; today, *technical* and *technique* can be applied to every facet of life. The Greek way of life was the embodied expression of a set of ideas and a system of values. Artistic production merely exemplified Greek virtues; indeed, the Greek gods themselves were virtues of heroic proportions. Temples were erected in the name of loyalty and honor, and plays were performed that dealt with justice and retribution.

The Greeks thought of art as a living experience. Aristotle believed that, "Art is produced when out of many ideas gained through experience we come to one general conclusion."[1] This presupposed a chasing after absolutes, and the "general conclusion" was never something one could hope to achieve. It remained forever subject to consensual revision lest it become an inbred doctrine. It was thought that there must always be something beyond, something that we strive for and seek after but are never 100 percent sure we know what it is. We must never fool ourselves into believing that our absolute values are "absolute." Believing that we have a monopoly on truth is a transgression against truth. By insisting on the verity of our ideas we are, in a way, preventing full disclosure, a requirement for any semblance of truth. Our values are based on a transcendent reality that we may desire but never actually have in our possession. However, values are unifying agents, the gratifying result of action in unison; they are causes for participation and the source of ethics. Whether we call our absolutes "God" or "beauty" or "truth" or "reason," they are expressions of humankind's ethical requirements. An ethic is disseminated, in part, through the aesthetic communication of ideas.

II

Art is a language; it communicates ideas. In this capacity we use art every day without ever thinking about it. Using the existing ideas in the world, we make new ideas of our own. There is art in the pages on which these words are written. Their usefulness—their utilitarian aspect—in containing and disseminating what has been printed on them is art. Any object, save inanimate ones, have this utilitarian feature. The utilitarian aspect of an *art* object is its ability to communicate an idea other than its own utility. We consider artists to be those who take this means of communication and use it as a tool for conveying a subjective message.

The utility of any object or device is completely different in nature from the idea being communicated by the artist. Artists' ideas mingle with their emotions, and their messages become inexplicably connected with their souls. This is art's subjective nature. But the art object must not entirely lose its utilitarian and pragmatic aspect. It must maintain its utility by being successfully communicated— by being understood—and it must be pragmatic by offering some benefit for those who engage in the communication. The ideas communicated by artists must somehow promise a brighter tomorrow. The artwork of successful artists is a fulfillment of the promise. Although each artist may be creating strictly for personal reasons, ultimately that body of production must be for the great weight of eternity that shall sit in judgment on these achievements.

Engaging in strictly utilitarian ideas is what separates artists from craftspeople. A room built by a carpenter has art on many levels.

The art in four walls is contained in the idea of the usefulness of that which is enclosed within. There is also the carpenter's art, i.e., the person's experience and knowledge of construction. However, the room itself is not a vehicle for further communication. The room is not an art object and therefore the carpenter craftsperson is not an artist.

Contemplation of strictly utilitarian ideas for their aesthetic qualities is the sign of an intellectual predisposition or short circuit. The car mechanic who can only appreciate the beauty of a purring engine is merely demonstrating the conditionality and limitations of an aesthetic awareness. However, the *art connoisseur* who sits in rapture while staring at four walls because the idea of the enclosed within, or the act of the craftsperson in creating, is considered worthy of artistic contemplation and engages in an intellectual vendetta against his own inability to enter in true aesthetic communication.

The language of aesthetic communication must be learned. Everyday we engage in aesthetic transactions when we communicate our thoughts and feelings. Most often we exchange our ideas verbally. The process we have undergone while learning our spoken language has committed to memory the understanding of the words. We speak and understand freely without reflecting on just how much art is involved in carrying on a conversation, whether it is the rudimentary grammatical structure, the turning of a clever phrase, or the profundity of our thought. Writers are artists who use the word as their creative material and their artwork is poetry and prose.

The practitioner of true aesthetic communication must be both artist and craftsperson. Just as carpenters must know their trade to construct a room, and auto mechanics must know how to make an engine purr, artists must possess certain technical skills in order to shape the materials of a chosen medium to perform their communicative role.

III

Techniques develop along lines of practicality. Methods that reach maximum effectiveness are practiced by the greatest number who collectively raise the quality of excellence through competition. The technical convention is the backdrop in front of which the real drama takes place. Here the artist uses the transcendental nourishment offered by technique to achieve self-becoming.

Technique is a necessary constituent in humankind's becoming in existence. Technique objectively represents resistance, against which human transcendence must persevere, namely, the ability to always do things better. Technique provides transcendental nourishment by demanding that a better way can be found—there is a promise of redemption. Any claim that one thing is better than another pre-supposes a system of values. Our values are based on ideal representations of reality. Technique provides for us a transcendental component, a fulcrum around which our transcendent selves find room in which to become.

In any endeavor, individual performance is measured in success or failure. Success is gauged by competently negotiating a system. It implies "know how." Technique is the cipher by which success is gauged. Being more successful means doing things better than the others. Technique provides a gridwork by which people can plan and achieve their goals. This transcendent vision of our future selves *is* our transcendent self. Those people who are successful technicians live their lives unconditionally by surpassing technique.

Techniques are conventions, substantive norms through or against which we conduct ourselves. Artists can choose between either complying or not complying with technical conventions. This is their fundamental right as free people. Whether they choose one way or another, if their choice was motivated by the fulfillment of their transcendental self, they have excercised unconditional choice. Self-becoming becomes objectified through technique. Artists become technique if they have been successful in adding to its greatest measure. Artists achieve a form of immortality by being so recognized by others.

IV

Unconditionality has been taken out of much artistic production. Art is no longer a communication between the one (the artist) and the many (fellow humans) engendered by a transcendental need for an eternal brotherhood. We have become spiritually separated from each other partially because we not longer communicate aesthetically in a coherent fashion.

Modern art claims that it is teaching new techniques of seeing and thinking about the world. Art is no longer viewed from a perspective that incorporates all the aesthetic components as a whole; instead, it claims that each part is an important element of the whole. Finding worth in the parts is certainly meritorious, but it is hedging the basic question: How do we bring intelligible unity into aesthetics?

When the artist's creative act is given credence as generating aesthetic value, we are confronted by a dilemma. How are we meant to understand that part of the whole being conveyed by the artist? We cannot identify as a "part" with the artist, because we are not the artist. We are our own "parts" and therefore different. It is by virtue of union in the whole that we as parts relate to each other, not by virtue of being parts that we claim unity as a whole. A part remains to a degree independent, while at the same time lacking independence. All other parts are similarly constituted, and what they are lacking may very well constitute the "partness" of other parts. When viewed from the perspective of the whole (in fact an adequate definition of "part" would necessitate it), communication of parts qua parts is untenable.

It is from the perspective of being a part of the whole that aesthetic communication becomes lucid and whole. The distinction between the part and the whole becomes clarified by the artist's communicative message. An artist whose message is so highly personal in nature that it expresses *his* "part" of reality has reduced the message to his own bare subjectivity. Each viewer must then approach the artwork on their own terms. They will only be able to judge by how it makes them feel in a most abstract sense. The more subjective the message, the more subjective the response. However, the idea has become objective, and it is across this objective threshold as an art object that the subjective message has been communicated. If the subjective message of the artist is unequivocal, this presupposes a unity and wholeness, something of which we all can feel a part has been expressed. The ability of the artist to communicate aesthetically is strictly determined by the extent to which we as participants in the communication find the artist's representation compelling in our own lives. The inspiration that gave birth to this communicative message is fleeting. We must therefore look to objectivity for clues to the nature of this psychic-physical phenomemon.

Is aesthetics simply an encyclopedia of unrelated facts, or does aesthetics have a transcendent reality by which it pursues a consistent path? Technique provides just such a path, which is traveled by the artist seeking unconditional self-becoming.

V

The meaning behind the idea, "being relative," is sweeping and ambiguous. During a heated conversation, someone may bring up an unrelated topic, to which the terse reply is made: "That is not relative." Or, two couples might go on a vacation. One couple likes to go shopping everyday, and go dining and dancing every night, while the other couple enjoys hiking through the woods and sitting around a campfire. It might be said that when it comes to enjoying life's pleasures, everything is "relative." These two interpretations of "relative" are contradictory. The former implies a "theory of relativity," that views things as adjoined and as having relations to one another. The latter suggests an independence among variables: that our ideas, and thus our values, are heterogeneous.

Values are not relative in this latter sense, they are homogeneous. If we do not establish standards of values, we cannot distinguish between right and wrong, and ethics would cease to exist. We construct our values upon a transcendent reality beyond finite possibilities: God, beauty, truth, and justice, are all in this transcendent domain. They are absolute articles of faith for those who believe in a transcendent reality. Reason, too, is an article of faith in a transcendent reality beyond our own, a reality in which everything is "right." When we appeal to our logic we are actually testing the fiber of our ethical character. The objective manifestations of this are the laws we create to govern our lives.

Ideas are different from values. We base our values on ideas, such as a perfect God, or equality. These ideas become the articles of faith upon which our values rest. Ideas are heterogeneous and transcendent realities. They conceive the world in complete fullness. Science, religion, jurisprudence, psychology, and even much of philosophy believe that the mechanics of their respective disciplines must operate as if by necessity. Any data that does not fit the established pattern is rejected or corrected. To the extent that the data fit the established pattern, the ideas emerging from them are viewed as reasonable. Philosophy is the most liberal of these ideal disciplines. It has recognized that reason itself is an article of faith, a transcendent reality with which our own reality must conform. The data of real existence are at times distorted and coerced to validate our preconceived ideas. Reason is therefore subject to human error.

In addition, modern philosophy has introduced the subjective reality of the act. Søren Kierkegaard's idea that "truth is subjectivity" leads (by way of Friedrich Nietzsche) to the belief that the subjective act is value generating. This created the illusion of relative values with relative truths. This was the essence of existentialism's error because it forgot that the idea itself was a transcendent reality, subject to error if we come to believe that our transcendent realities have actually been arrived at in any objectified form. Action may be the seat of transcendence, but acts are not objects.

Our senses and thoughts respond intuitively as a total sensory apparatus. Intuition is the bedrock upon which reason rests. Should intuition be questioned? Intuition is accompanied by a feeling of certainty. This feeling of certainty is based on what we recognize as the two irreducible contingencies of existence—time and space. We have access to space by means of our body. We have access to time by means of our consciousness. Time is simply a mechanized concept of conscious reality. The scientific idea of conscious reality has contaminated our reasoning capacities in every discipline. Here lies reason's road to darkness. We delight in creating ideal parodies of ourselves and putting them on display like cultural exhibitions at the museum of natural history. We label them philosophy, sociology, psychology, anthropology, religion, history, science, humanities, with countless subdivisions. We find ourselves at a distance from these disciplines because we are living and they have become ossified ornaments and fossils.

The answer to whether intuition can be considered credible rests in recognizing three things: the transcendent self as the fulcrum around which time and space converge; that the transcendent self is not something ever arrived at, because once objectified it looses its quality of being transcendent; and that all of our ideas are also transcendent and in a continual state of flux. This presents the image of a dialectic without end and without purpose. Science and religion have resisted this image, yet each falls victim to its own reasonable component. Society becomes blind to those things that our strictest laws and rules declare do not exist.

It is from within the circle of the human transcendent self that all becoming in existence originates. Our projects become the world. Ideas originate as a task put before us to achieve. They are brought to fruition through action. In this way all objectivity can be considered as the disclosure of transcendence, but not as transcendence itself. Transcendence is a process, a becoming, of the transmutation from subjective affectivity to the objective.

VI

The potential for oil paint to convey retinal imagery is unlimited. This is the same as saying that human potential is unlimited. The concept of technique provides us with the transcendent element for achieving our potential. The paint itself is inert. It has characteristics, such as transparency, opaqueness, color intensity, body, etc. It does not have potential any more than a flint and steel have the potential for combining to make a fire. The spark produced is a characteristic of its physical properties.

Potential is realized after an action is taken to produce a desired end. Potential presupposes a conscious effort to acquire. We first recognize our potential as a possibility, and then realize that potential through action. The potential becomes the actual. This is the process of becoming in existence. By recognizing our potential we project our transcendent selves into a situation. Our transcendent selves have an infinite potentiality. The self beyond the self is our most haunting aspect. It taunts. We can either accept these visions of ourselves and pursue our becoming in existence, or we can lose confidence in our ability to manage the situation in a transcendentally gratifying way.

Technique has potential with respect to the measure of the individual. A potential unrealized is a transcendental failure and assumes a negative quality. This negativity can haunt as well, breaching the void from nothingness to remind individuals of their failure. It becomes the situation beyond their control and an object of constant despair. Realizing our potential is an apotheosis with our transcendental selves.

VII

Success in any field, regardless of the merit of the product or service, takes intelligence and hard work in coping with a system. A law of selection is at work that produces a pyramid-like structure in society. The most powerful and successful represent the pinnacle and must be considered more singular in their achievements. This law of "natural selection," is put forth by libertarians and the evolutionists. It does not necessarily represent either a strengthening or weakening of humankind's metaphysical adhesion. Nietzsche claimed that natural selection produced exactly the opposite that it predicted: not a strengthening of the species, but a dissolution of ethical solidarity.[2] From the point of view of Nietzsche's spirituality, he was right. However, Nietzsche failed to recognize how overpowering materialism was to become within the matrix of our lives, with ourselves as prisoners to a techno-industrial landscape of our own making.

This aspect of our unique achievement is paradoxically two sided. On the one hand, it represents a level of achievement that singles out individuals as having performed their respective tasks more successfully than others; on the other hand, it can represent the ability to communicate with an audience on a one-to-one level, of providing for a need that is singular in its universality. Immense wealth could lie in store for someone who is able to provide most efficiently a basic necessity that everyone requires: in other words, the person who can build the proverbial better mouse trap. If the effort expended is successful and the material need is provided, we are rewarded with material satisfaction. By the same token, those who can supply the spiritual needs of a multitude will receive in return spiritual benefits. These spiritual benefits are an ethical community of love for fellow citizens. It is the job of aesthetic communication to reveal a "gospel" of social harmony and love.

VIII

Art is the communication of ideas. Aesthetic communication is involved in areas outside that which would strictly be called artistic. There is utilitarian art, the objects of which communicate their usefulness to us as we use them. The utilitarian idea is an aesthetic idea because its use is determined by practice toward a desired end. The "desired end" can in every way be likened to Aristotle's "general conclusion." Aesthetic communication is learning to do better through experience.

Artists are inventors. Much like novelists, they must find ways of abstracting from daily experiences the underlying drama that goes unnoticed. It goes unnoticed because we, the actors, are too psychologically close to the situation to free ourselves from our egocentric perspective, and because many of our once-learned behaviors have become habituated into unconscious structural mechanisms.

Artists must invent new ways of looking at the world. In this respect their inventiveness is displayed as a rabid curiosity: they may become obsessed with the configurations of leaves, trees, and clouds. The preoccupation with rocks may rival that of a geologist. Or the artist may choose the ponderings of the human mind as a subject for investigation. The caliber of the artist's inventiveness will be gauged not by the research topic, but by the effect the research has on the existing body of knowledge.

Leonardo da Vinci is the best example of the close link between artist and inventor, and is indeed the person for whom the descriptive term "Renaissance man," was coined. Leonardo was a serious painter who studied in the workshop of Verrochio, yet for Leonardo painting always remained a hobby. His real interest lay in inventing machines, particularly war machines, and in the studying of nature. He has left us a far greater record of the range of his mind in these fields than in painting. Yet his few surviving paintings are considered the greatest treasures in all art history.

When an artist intends to use a medium to communicate some message, the profundity of his thought is not measured by the amount of knowledge or special training put into it, but by the extent to which the production has altered the way we conceive of the body of knowledge as a whole. If we now think of the knowledge in terms of this production, it has attained a transcendental significance. It has crossed over into that body of "general conclusions" and "desired ends."

The truly great and enduring artistic achievements have been when gifted and inventive individuals realize through technique the means to accomplishments deserving of the title "genius." Even outside art, we measure genius by the breadth of application. The contributions of Newton, Goethe, and Einstein are all-encompassing. They touch every facet in their field. They have been the objects of ridicule and still maintain the vouchsafed mantle of affirmation.

Few artists have been afforded the opportunity to achieve this type of transcendental significance, and then only when the aesthetic communication on both the ethical and technical side provided the circumstance in which it could happen. In other words, when the values expressed are of an all-embracing and unifying nature, and when the prevailing technical means are ripe for exploitation. Some of the artists whose achievements could be counted among the geniuses are: Raphael, Titian, Michelangelo, Rembrandt, Vermeer, Goya, Cezanne, and Picasso.

IX

To what heights might our ideas aspire? The utilitarian might answer, "to bringing the greatest benefit to the greatest number." The theologian might imply the very same idea when he simply states the word, "God." The scientist likewise thinks the same thing when he says, "to achieve an explainable order by which things happen by necessity." What these three interpretations have in common is harmony. These concepts of harmony offer assurance and peace of mind; they are like stars affixed in a firmament of confusion, ignorance, misunderstanding, and error.

The qualities of harmony are as truly cosmological as are the stars in the sky. Harmony transcends every disconcerted aspect of life by providing a peace-giving, a predictable atmosphere. The harmony found in a musical composition, in a painting, in the precision parts of a mechanical device, or, most particularly, the harmony among human beings imparts a sense of tranquility and beneficence.

Ideas that aspire to a transcendent future must promise ultimate redemption, i.e., the benefits of participation in a better tomorrow. Philosophy, religion, science, and the arts, all make this claim either explicitly or implicitly. However, the promise is never one that can be fulfilled. The ideas we live by may have honorable intentions, but the transcendent realities are never attained. They always remain at a distance; their achievement remaining something to work toward. The faith we maintain in our transcendental ideas is our justification for living and for participating with others in common activities.

Participation is one of the great positive forces human beings engage in. There is great comfort in the idea that we are all human beings and all embarking on the same basic activities of life. We participate in choosing our leaders, constructing the laws we live by, and playing games. A life without participation and cooperation would be bitter, unhappy, and devoid of hope.

Technique is what unites participation with achievement. When people participate, procedural standards are established, and those procedures bringing the most successful results are practiced by the greatest number of people. By means of competition standards of excellence continue to rise. This is true in any field, from fishing to engineering, from gardening to painting. The greatest of human achievements have occurred when talented people, using the available techniques at their disposal, raised the level of technique to new heights and thereby raised the level of excellence for everyone.

X

Art has undergone a process of transformation that would have been impossible to predict. It is no more possible to determine the course of art than it is to predict the course of our species. Both are inextricably bound to the human "being," to our processes of becoming. We may attempt to comment on art's "existence," on the physical manifestations of art, but art's transcendental process of becoming is always beyond our grasp.

A historical approach to art enables us to track its course. Art history is a record of humankind's metaphysical reconciliation of its ideas with the objective world. Art history gives concrete examples of our attitudes toward our own existence and, more importantly, it defines the place of the human species in the broader scheme of things. A cursory overview of art history might conclude that, initially, human beings used art to make tangible the ideas and values that sprang from our "intelligible" capacities: art represented the flowering of human capacities which aspire to unity. Art then took a giant step sideways in an attempt to create the necessary distance required for reflection. In this way art became severed from the center of human existence and took the position of an outsider looking in. An apt description of this metamorphosis would be that there was a shift from art as "representation" of human transcendence to art as "description," or "explanation," of that same process of becoming. However, by alienating itself from the center of existence, namely, from transcendence, this modern tendency has achieved exactly the opposite of what it intended. It made objective that which can never be objectified—human transcendence—and thereby closed itself off from life experiences.

Alienation is the major constituent in art's current expression of how we conceive of ourselves. This may be the unavoidable consequence of an all-consuming and depersonalized technological order. Material gain has encouraged us to surround ourselves with our own private paradises, while cutting ourselves off from others. Aesthetic estrangement is the inevitable result of this spiritual separation. Aesthetic estrangement and spiritual separation are both symptoms of the same infectious malady: an egocentricism that cuts us off from others. It is only through our understanding of others that we can truly come to an understanding of ourselves. It is by means of unity through the whole that aesthetic communication aspires to achieve a true ethical community.

This is one reason why technique has become such a catalytic force in modern society, and at the same time a concept denigrated and denied for its part in supplying transcendental nourishment for our becoming in existence. We vehemently deny that the technological order has taken over, that we now serve that which was created to serve us. We have become drones in our computerized world and would be helpless should anyone "pull the plug." Our ability to rise above reason has been supplanted by the view of ourselves as mere parts of the process, much like our own digestive or reproductive systems are simply parts—however vital—of a structural apparatus in an organism.

All of these changes in our existence in no way alters the nature of our becoming, or of art's role of clarifying the human component in existence. These changes point up that we are no longer captains of the ship. Technique as such has not been altered, only exiled. It's potential has been sapped only because we have lost confidence in our own potential. We are unwilling to risk failure and, "not live up to our potential." Every significant act thrusts ahead into the unknown against the chance of failure. By refusing to take responsibility for ourselves, we forfeit our chance for a better tomorrow. We have chosen to mortgage our spiritual future in return for material contentment today.

NOTES

1. Aristotle, *Metaphysics* (New York: Walter J. Black, 1943).

2. Friedrich Nietzsche, *Twilight of the Idols* (London: Penguin Books, 1968), "Expeditions of an Untimely Man," #14.

6

The Technique of Painting

Sight is the most compelling of our senses . . . "seeing is believing."
Sounds and smells may conjure up nostalgic memories of the past,
but sight is verification of what is here and now. That is why people
have always sought to visualize the workings of their minds. Even
in our dreams the pictorial process takes place.

The development of painting techniques are intrinsic to the inherent properties of oil-based paint. The intention was didactic: to
create an appearance, an illusion of reality, to some idea of which
the painting was a representation. The work of art was not a presen-
tation, but a *re*-presentation. The painting was a facsimile of the
idea, once removed from the picture the artist might have had in
mind, and perhaps twice removed from the original inspiration that
moved the artist. The inspiration of an artist is fleeting and it is
doubtful that such inspiration could be explained in objective terms.

The creative act of the artist unites inspiration with the image
that assembles in his or her reflective mind to produce the art object.
The fact that the object represents some idea the artist has is directly
connected with the technique of pursuing an "ideal" manner of
representation. This becomes the means of communication.

The subjective message must be carried by the object. The art
object is a catalyst for subjective responses. It is in objectivity that
the perceiver's subjective "buttons" are pushed. It is therefore in
objectivity that we must search for the manner and meaning of the
subjective response. This is where object and subject join along the
boundaries of negation, representing the great paradox of art, namely,
that subjectivity must assume its metaphysical opposite in order to

be communicated to another. It therefore relies on our common sense of objectivity.

All artworks are in their own way "realities," things that exist. A clever thought is, in its own way, a work of art; and if it remains unstated by its author, it does retain a significance for its lonely audience of one. Artists achieve significance to the degree that they are able to reach and move their audiences. Aesthetic communication is a language, and some artists and art perceivers may be more fluent in one technique than another. Some are able to master the difficulties of a rigorous technique, while others are not.

The classical ideal is one of many and perhaps the most narrowly circumscribed. It therefore offers artists the least latitude in transcending technique. The slightest deviation from the convention represents a radical departure from the norm. The limitations imposed by convention build strength in the artist. Artists test the tenets of a convention like archers test a bow. The tighter bow will hurl the projectile farther. The bow provides resistance. It can be bent just so far until it breaks. In like manner, the convention provides just such resistance for the artist. The technical convention is an objective means by which progress can be judged.

Success or failure is measured through technique. There is no success without the risk of failure. Failure presupposes something lost across objectivity. There cannot be a subjective failure. We may fail our friends and family, but even this involves technique in the conduct of our lives. Technique is an objective manifestation of change. This is its transcendent nature.

If we accept a transcendent technique, a problem immediately arises. Once accepted, it crosses into the hoary objectivity of existence, subject to all the intellectual fabrications that history presents to us. How do we fix something that must by definition remain always unfixed? The transcendental quality of technique refuses to allow technique to stand still. Therefore we must look to the objective manifestations of technique as our signposts of progress. Transcendence must always spring from the stream of objective existence.

Painting techniques must be enumerated by analyzing the skills necessary for artists to successfully communicate their message. "Skill" should not in anyway be understood to mean pure mechanical dexterity. It is the mind that moves the impulses that animate both our emotions and our nervous mechanisms.

The technical components of painting did not come together solely to satisfy the requirements of representation. Great artists are recognized by the manner in which they use these components and the effect they have on us as participants in the communicative act. There is a "reason" why the contours employed by an artist can create a chilling stir in our fiber: those who experience art have spoken out to say to the artist that "this technique is a way to communicate."

Techniques in painting gravitate toward two poles: the "graphic," and the "pictorial." These two terms have assumed an ambiguity of meaning because of their application in various fields. Violence, or sexual content, can be "graphic" in being explicit. A photo layout is also called a "pictorial," and when applied to painting, pictorial is sometimes associated with "pastoral," bucolic scenes.

Technically, in painting, the "graphic" is concerned with the linear quality of a work of art: more specifically, the manner in which line and contour are conveyed. The "pictorial" is associated with the painterly. A more linear treatment is pursued by classicism, and a painterly finish is more conducive to a romantic or expressionistic conception.

Also, under the term "graphic" is generally implied drawings and prints, although these can employ a wide range of representational methods, from the linear to the painterly. For our purposes, "graphic" will refer primarily to the quality of conveying imagery by line and contour, particularly in drawings and prints, and the pictorial will refer to the rendering of atmospheric and tactile properties, most often through a conditioning of line, contour, and color. Expressive qualities can be achieved using all manner of representation, from the lyrical sweep of Botticelli's line to the cold and hard-edged beauty of Ingres's stony embrace to the dynamic penetration of Van Gogh's contorted brushstrokes.

The technique of oil painting is embodied in the possession of certain "illusionistic" devices. These devices are: composition, line, contour, color, light, design, and brushstroke. Composition is the premiere component in painting.

The conventional definition of composition is the ordering of objects in space, in an illusionistic space on the canvas. This raises an important question: Does a nonobjective painting have composition? Strictly speaking, space is the prerequisite for objects to exist, and the existence of an object presupposes space. Therefore a nonobjective painting does not have a composition as we have defined it. However, if the grouping of nonobjective forms are arranged to create balance or weight in the painting—balance and weight being characteristics of objectivity—there has been the implication of space, and therefore the painting has composition.

A composition can convey serenity, agitation, or indifference. This will be determined by the emphasis created when the compositional elements are arranged. The composition must lead the eye along a path of visual events. This is a part of the experience of art. We "meet" the work of art, and it can either take us through the exhilaration of expectation and fulfillment, or it can be utterly boring. The boredom or exhilaration we experience at viewing an artwork will be determined by two things: the success of the artist at communicating an idea, and the extent to which we as participants in the communication find the message compelling in our own lives. These two determinants are irresistibly connected in a single expression. The closest word to describe this synthesis might be *acknowledgment,* however that falls far short of explaining the intuitive character of this intersubjective communication.

Composition is the abode of the artist's sense of order. However, whether that home is immaculate or a mess does not necessarily reflect on the profundity of the artist's statement. It will, however, affect the artist's ability to communicate a message. A message untold or unsuccessfully told is lost. Building a good composition requires solid command of one's craft, like a carpenter building a house; it also requires imagination, like that of the architect who is forever imagining new and useful ways of building houses.

There is a distinction that must be made between a painting's composition and its design. Design is the outward framework of a painting, composition is its inner gravity. A painting is held together by its composition, design is a surface embellishment. Two paintings can have the same composition and yet project entirely different designs, simply by substituting one object for another. A painting can contain objects that are frilly and ornamental, or the objects can be solid and streamlined. The manner will become part of the expressive quality of the work as a whole, either gay or somber. If the composition is successful in achieving its communicative mission, it will be successful in either of these examples.

The qualities of line in a painting or drawing can be compared to the melodic line in music: It can be lyrical, presenting gentle cadences; circumlocutious, carrying us to dizzying heights; erratic, leading to agitation; or bold like bombast. Line gives direct evidence of the intuitive character of the artist's expression. There are deep implications for the manner in which line is employed. A line can be either certain or uncertain: this is determined by how observers meet and participate with the line. If a straight line is drawn from point A to point B, this illustration contains all the ramifications of our entire concept of space, motion, and time. Without any training in physics, we as participants are still able to meet and travel along that line, with all its metaphysical implications, on an intuitive level.

The certainty of a line is something intuitively known. An ambient line may be whimsical, lighthearted, and airy, without ever touching solid ground. Creating lighthearted and airy lines that are amorphous does not require the training needed to focus oneself on the solid ground. Such lines are haphazard and uncertain. While a line may be light and airy, it must also have a toehold in objectivity.

Line adds "hard-edged" definition to a painting, or, inversely, it can be softened to a haze. It can be dynamic or static. Line is an "unruly" element in art. It offers the artist a full spectrum of expression, and also hides the most serious pitfalls and snags. Line can timidly submit, or conquer. If line is being used by the artist as a means to further and better communicate a message, line is subservient. If line serves no message, but has become the message, line has conquered.

Color is expressive of our moods. Colors do not reflect a true visual equivalent of our moods, but adopt a certain colloquial meaning through implication and habitual use. We talk of something "coloring our moods." We feel blue, or in the pink. When something makes us mad it's like, "waving a red flag." These associations have real objective validity. They have value for their symbolic representation of real experiences. People from completely different upbringings will find paintings done in pastel blues and grays to be "cool," and will find paintings done in orange and lush reds "warm." These color associations find their genesis directly in experience. A parched and arid landscape will be comprised of ochers, umber, and grey. An icy wilderness will be bathed in a shocking blue-white. Swelter is characterized by deep greens and lush reds.

The colors of our surroundings make an immediate impression

on our mood. The interior of a hospital is white, impersonal, and cold. A fire truck is alarmingly red, while the red of our own blood is instrumental in establishing the power of red to condition our emotions.

There is an undulation of color associated with habitat: being in harmony and tranquil within our homes and within ourselves. We arrange our homes to be "color coordinated," and we immediately recognize when something clashes. There is a music among compatable colors, it affects us as does any harmony. The development of color sense is learned. Anything expressed intuitively in this fashion is linguistic, a way of communicating that has its origin in the deepest memories of our collective consciousness.

Color presents artists with different avenues of approach. Initially, artists filled in their outlines with "pure color." This created a cut-out appearance. Artists later learned to model color with light and shadow by conditioning the intensity of the color value, or brightness. Then they discovered that objects tended to take on the color of their surroundings. Paintings softened to a patchwork of "local color." Whatever the approach, artists always operate contingent upon the existing historical body of color technique. Even the color field painters of today are responding to what is an existing convention.

Contour is the component in painting that cleaves most arduously to objectivity. Objects have shapes, and contour is the representation of these shapes. Contour can be considered within the context of geometric abstraction. Cubes and spheres have edges beyond outlines. Strictly speaking, contour is three dimensional: it presupposes space and objectivity. Circles and lines do not have contours; they have shape but no depth. Their arrangement can go into the ordering of a composition or design and they can even be grouped in perspective according to size to create the illusion of depth, but this is not a contour. Contour has no place in "autonomous" abstraction.

The preponderance of contour is akin to that of line; it can be either certain or uncertain. That depends on the axiomatic plausibility of the object in question. Artists take great pains in conveying their objects in accordance with our intuitions about space and our sensory knowledge about objects. The most obvious technique involving contour is that of foreshortening, which creates the illusion that a part of the object lies hidden from view behind that which is seen. The importance of this technique was recognized two millennia ago by Pliny in his treatise on painting.

A contour can be either hard-edged and defined, ragged and ambiguous, or evanescent as if emerging from fog. Whatever its outward manifestation, contour must remain firmly grounded in the objective world. Like the tenets of representation itself, contour must retain its axiomatic certainty. Taken beyond this point, the equilibrium established by our intuition snaps.

It is the duty of the artist to convey contour convincingly. The artists' contours may be expressive and unexpected, but never unconvincing. The greatest expression through contour is demonstrated in the work of El Greco (1548–1614). Here all is in flux, a give and take of substance and form. The very air around El Greco's figures seems to merge with the objects they surround. Contours are piled upon contours to a dizzying crescendo. Our equalibrium is subjected to a kind of vertigo all kept in check by the powerful and mysterious quality of El Greco's apotheosis with his artistic vision.

Brushstrokes are as personal as handwriting. No two are alike. The greatest forger could not duplicate the sensitivity of an expressive brushstroke. Facile brushworking enlivens a painting with spontaneity. Brushstroke is the component of painting that is most closely dependent on manual dexterity. But brushstrokes express much more than simple mechanical skills. They offer direct evidence of the nervous mechanisms animating through the artist's fingertips. The brush is an instrument for directly engaging those impulses and giving them objective expression. Blending expressive brushstrokes on a canvas is a cathartic experience for an artist. There is an air of exploration rising on the hope of discovery. An artist's identity can take shape on the canvas, a permanent home for the person's transcendent spirit.

This process of artists finding themselves is tied directly to their sensory perception apparatus. It finds expression through eye and hand coordination. Native skills can take artists only so far. Eye and hand coordination is engaged by each person's data bank of learned knowledge. When this has reached its capacity for expression, the brushstroke technique offers an avenue of progress, a next step. Technique offers guidance and confidence.

Brushstrokes can be intimidating as well. Instead of offering a next step, they can just as easily "draw a line," daring the artist to cross. All significant achievements in the technique of painting have been at the risk of that dare.

Two other mechanical components are available to artists as aids in their communication. They are lighting and perspective. The rediscovery of scientific perspective in the Renaissance set the stage for single-point perspective for centuries to come. Prior to the Renaissance, Gothic painters delighted in juxtaposing weird angles in unexpected ways. The Gothic painters were scorned by their Renaissance heirs as untrained and barbaric. The Renaissance mind was constituted by an ideal immersed in rational humanism, and could not identify with the ecstatic Gothic sentimentality.

Perspective can be incorporated into a composition to create dramatic emphasis. The first to exploit perspective in this manner was Andrea Mantegna (1431–1506), who's compositions are highly original for this reason. Perspective can also be used in a "sensational" manner, like a transfiguration rising to a heavenly abode.

Perspective is significant in the construction of a landscape. The placement of the horizon in relation to the top and bottom of the painting will determine the perspective of the viewer. It will place the viewer at the height of the horizon: a horizon low on the painting will place the viewer on a low-lying plain, while a horizon at the top of the painting finds the viewer in lofty heights. Whatever the placement, perspective in a landscape must instill a sense of surroundings, even if distant and cold, a sense of place where the viewer can imagine being.

Perspective can also be used to create an optical illusion. These paintings create a hybrid space out of sorts with our own conceptions. Such optical illusions make interesting visual exercises; they disclose to the viewer their own sense of place by exposing them to others.

Light and shade can also be used by artists to create dramatic emphasis. These effects were discovered by the early baroque masters and were used to create a variety of expressive qualities, from the piously humble to the brassy and theatrical.

Light has been a preoccupation with all painters since the seventeenth century and at times has become an obsession. Light has been given every conceivable source, both earthbound and heavenly. Impressionists were guided by a scientific belief that an object's surface was constituted visually by color and light. They believed that oil paint contained the required properties to depict this diffuse and permeable cloak of form-giving substance. The impressionists came up with many interesting visual documents; however, they never actually accomplished their goals. Because of their preoccupation with the manner in which light was conveyed they developed a technique confined to their particular approach. The result was a nontranscendent, stereotyped style. Impressionistic light has become the most "ideal" representation, far from how anything actually looks. Today, the impressionist ideal pales into a curious experiment.

Successful light does not depend on the self-conscious manner in which light is used. It does not search for an explanation of light's characteristics. Light is successful through what it is used to express. Light is life giving. It reveals what lurks in shadows; it provides security and safe haven in darkness. Light is reassurance and contentment. These attributes do not emanate from the painting's subject matter, but from how the subject is disclosed to the viewer. It can bathe its objects in caressing warmth, or shock with terrible brilliance. What counts is not the reflection of light as it traces across the surface of objects, but how it fills the spaces between objects, how it transcends that physical distance and creates a space that can be entered, where the artist's message can breathe the fresh air of a new day.

These techniques of painting are only tools. Their effectiveness depends on our ingenuity. Their noble and enduring qualities depend on our intuition. A technique *is* effective by appealing to intuition. Aesthetic communication assumes an obligation to present things in a way that is effective and noble. Technique offers a challenge to always find new ways to communicate.

7

Masters of Technique

INTRODUCTION

The number of subjects to paint and the ways to paint them are limited only by the artist's imagination. This includes the familiar representation of objects with sensory qualities. We recognize an apple as red by our sense of sight, and we recognize silk as soft by our sense of touch. This also includes objects with which we are not visually familiar—i.e., objects of thought. How do we color an emotion? Is depression blue and envy green? Describing an abstract emotion nonobjectively is purely subjective. Is it also arbitrary?

There is no line between the abstract and the objective. Each has a reciprocal component of the other. When objectivity approaches the plane of pure idealism it is underlined with abstract formulas resembling geometric equations. When representation dissolves into subjective abstraction, there must likewise be some common element upon which to base our subjective response. Otherwise the artistic production is truly arbitrary. It all comes down to the artist's message, its applicability to our concerns, and to the artist's ability at making the message understood.

Artists use all manner of ways to convey their messages visually. The content of images are not restricted to descriptive or narrative form. The art can be suggestive through the way it is constructed. An abstract "action" painting is invested with a pretext of "process" and "gesture." Or, subject matter can be conditioned to create irony or allegory. The ability of the artist to communicate is conditioned by the subjective response of those who participate

101

in the communication. It relies on the common element of objectivity for comprehension.

Artists adopt a wide spectrum of representational vehicles to carry their communication, but most fall into three general categories: figure, landscape, and still life. Each of these seek to express our metaphysical need to channel that forward rush of our transcendence into objective terms. These terms are the objective manifestation of existence, and their presence represents our conquering spirit.

The artist conquers space by painting the human body. The body is our direct access to objectivity. All objective manifestations get their orientation by way of the body. Painters of the figure truly play the part of perfecter. They have taken a great gamble and have cast their fate to the future hoping that their vision will pass into the annuls of continuing excellence and recognition. The painting has a life of its own. The life of the artist's work beyond the life of the artist is nourished on pure transcendence. Its continuing survival is strictly conditioned by events in the future, by the extent to which future generations accept the artist's vision as their own.

The figure painter depends on anatomy. There is no "perfect" anatomy that the artist can rely on. The closer one gets to an ideal type the further the representation looks like any real individual. The more the image resembles a specific type, the further it gets from common characteristics. The artist must search for the specific in the universal: not the universal that tends toward the common and ideal physiognomy, but the specific quality that makes us all brothers and sisters—a positive and hopeful tomorrow. The artist accomplishes this through technique by demonstrating new kinships in anatomy. This is achieved through the conditioning, distorting, and abstracting of the generic anatomical forms. The distortion can be taken only to the limits of the axiomatic plausibility of the body. Beyond that our intuitions are given a jolt that something it not right. A man cannot walk straight if one leg is twelve inches shorter than the other.

The painter of still life is attempting to harness real transience or the fleeting surface of things, the natural cycle of life, death, and rejuvenation—the urge to capture a moment. Still life is intimately involved with time. There are many ways to express the meaning of "time." Science adopts a "stopwatch" mentality explaining time as something that moves like the hands of a clock. This is a thoroughly objective description and completely excludes the subjective reality of time as conscious reality, the recognition that our consciousness persists.

All reality exists manifestly in "immediate" time. One immediate is mediated by the next to produce an implied succession. However, this succession is never something traversed, like a measured mile. When aesthetic communication travels centuries between an artwork and its admirer, it is across conscious reality that the message is received.

When some artists choose still life as their object of aesthetic contemplation they gamble more than the figure painter in trying to produce an enduring message. They choose the ephemeral trappings of their surroundings, things most prone to obsolescence. In addition, the still life itself can become obsolete. When this happens the painting is rendered fatuous. An object, or a painting, becomes obsolete for the same basic reasons: either something better came along, or the original was of little value to begin with.

The transcendental significance of a still life never resides in the transitory quality of yesterday's objects, but in the effectiveness of the artist at capturing the ephemeral quality forever "now" as a representation on a canvas. This involves technique. The impression of having succeeded in capturing the "essence" of the subject is achieved in doing it in a new and better way.

Landscape is an appeal to provident management. A statement that the land is a common bond uniting all people. A successful landscape will communicate an affinity that all people have. The whole of humankind rose from a common origin—Mother Earth. However, the Earth has become "uncommon." The ground is scarred with boundaries painted in blood, separating what is ours from what is theirs. We have come to think of the land as our personal possession. This belief leads to "national pride." It was during just such periods that landscape found its greatest expression, particularly in Holland during the seventeenth century, and in the United States during the nineteenth century.

We can never own the land. The names we put on maps will be scattered like dust across the winds of time to join the great civilizations of the past. Landscape must continually remind us of that past, not by telling us stories that no longer have any meaning in our lives, but by revealing some hidden aspect of that nature of which we all feel a part. A landscape must express eternity, otherwise it is reduced to mere history.

The eternal union of all human beings is expressed as nature in harmony with itself. This is a great metaphor for humanity at peace. A landscape painting represents humankind as the creator of this harmony.

Painting techniques have developed and changed since their inception. The rudiments of painting have been taken through a remarkable course by such extraordinary people as Raphael, Michelangelo, Titian, Vermeer, Rembrandt, Goya, Cezanne, and Picasso. Their paintings represent the concrete manifestations of technique's transcendent life. The achievements of these painters are significant, for the influence their work had on the evolution of the mechanics of painting, and for the influence their careers had on the course of art history.

CLASSICISM

Raphael—Michelangelo—Titian

Raphael represents the culmination of a system that took over one hundred years to develop. Does perfection also encompass innovation? The two ideas appear mutually exclusive. How can what is just now being created anew be perfected? That can only be the work of a "God." Raphael is not a creator, but a perfector. His hard-won achievement was in using the means at his disposal to do better what others had done before. The work of Raphael towers above that of his contemporaries through the subtleties and nuances that gave such compelling weight to the tenets of classical painting. The harmonies of ideal balance in form and color are not far removed from his peers, and yet they are in a world apart.

Raphael's paintings fulfill all the requirements of the classical ideal: they are fine and noble. If they intrigue and excite it is not because of content or an explicit manner by which the elements are given an expressive quality. It is via the unified gravity that is created by the solid construction. The paintings are characterized by a "correctness." Raphael worked with the benefit of all of the advances made during the fifteenth century. Composition, color, anatomy, and perspective were grafted onto each other into the amalgam of the classical ideal. These advances in technique sat perched upon the crown of artistic development, ready and assembled. Raphael was the right man who came along at the right time to unite his own native skills with the techniques at hand. That his skills were considerable is demonstrated by the heights to which he took painting in the Renaissance.

Classicism as an ideal worthy of the artist's pursuit has appeared and reappeared since antiquity. The classical ideal is based on a bias toward representation, or "reality." Yet that ideal can become so ideal that it is far removed from how things are actually presented in nature or "reality." This is particularly true of the classical ideal when it becomes attached to a theological conception of a mythological character. It is an ideal conception and no longer real.

One of the characteristics of Renaissance painting is a smooth finish, blended and polished to the luster of alabaster. The nervous mechanisms of the artist's facility and impulses were not allowed to assert themselves by means of an expressive brushstroke. These impulses were sublimated and found release in the coordination of the painting's formal elements: composition, color, line, and contour. The artist's emotions were kept in check and restricted to expressing themselves within the tension created by these elements, or more precisely, the tension of maintaining a balance between these elements. Michelangelo and Titian were the first to exploit this great pressure cooker of tension held in check within the bounds of classicism.

Michelangelo was a man of extremes. He was temperamental, defiant, worldly and ambitious. He was small in physical stature, but a giant among artists. Michelangelo was able to add expressive significance to the classical ideal of anatomy by bringing to it the dignity of the humanist. In comparison, the sculptures of antiquity are cold and removed.

Michelangelo was the product of a system that produced artists to perform a pedagogical function. Artistic production was strictly circumscribed to elucidate the virtues of the church and state—a type of propaganda. Technique was controlled by a system of guilds that disseminated procedure and were themselves beholden to their secular and ecclesiastical patrons. In this respect artists were still considered a class of craftspeople. The power of the artist's personality was held in check by the strict rigidity of convention. The towering heights achieved by the Renaissance masters were a product of the spirit of competition nurtured by humanism, aided by the strict control imposed by technique.

Michelangelo was the first to assert the power of his personality against this system. It was the strength and severity of this system that made him strong and severe. This change of direction is most tellingly displayed in the Sistine Chapel, perhaps the most spectacular accomplishment of any artist. The anatomical distortions created by Michelangelo were completely unprecedented. They represent a kinetic release of a powerful reserve trapped within the classical ideal. Contrary to contemporary modes of thought, which ask, "To what heights might Michelangelo have risen had he been free of the shackles of convention?" it is only by means of his resistance against the techniques and conventions of his day that such supreme heights could have been reached.

Michelangelo's *David* is an example of how a technical convention can be lifted to new heights by the resistance of the artist to break through the bonds of the convention. *David* is an image of composure and repose. Underneath is masked a drama of tension and defiance. It is Michelangelo himself straining at the limits of classicism. *David* is a cry for compassion: "I am human, I am not just an ideal abstraction." *David* is more real than his ideal predecessors. He is more real because of his psychological identity, which is an expression of Michelangelo the man. It is the beginning of a true intersubjective message and it has been achieved via technique. In this respect Michelangelo can be considered the great-grandfather of modern art. His art takes on the character of a subjective message. This is the characteristic of all the great masters in whose work we discern an "identity."

Titian invented brushstrokes. Some claim that it was merely the aging master's failing eyesight that transformed the flush picture surface into a painterly one. This would discredit Titian's towering accomplishment of recognizing and exploiting the attributes of local color, and of conveying through the oil medium an intuitive depiction of tactile qualities.

The Venetians were ahead of their Renaissance colleagues in the practice of painting in oils by virtue of their close contact with the north of Europe. They were already painting on canvas while their Florentine contemporaries were still painting on boards. Canvas provided a far superior ground and offered a gentle give beneath the impulses animated through the artist's brush or knife. A board offers too resilient a support and asserts its own rigidity across the surface of the painting. A board is more suited to a linear treatment while a canvas gives sway to more variegated pictorialization.

Titian made giant strides in representing tactile qualities. His Renaissance contemporaries still created their paintings in a linear fashion of solid color and outline. Leonardo's diffuse *sfumato* was basically an atmospheric effect that still left a smooth and flush picture surface as prescribed by convention. Titian's approach is tactile. He is concerned with the surface of things, and he is the first to truly exploit and incorporate the tactile qualities of the paint and canvas themselves in conveying this illusion. Here, for the first time, wonderful new terrain is discovered. The discoveries of the potential inherent in oil paint to represent images visually must have been as exciting as the discoveries of "new lands" going on at the same time.

The breakdown of the picture surface to mimic tactile qualities naturally lead to the breakdown of the classical composition defined by symmetrical order, and here Titian again leads the way. His compositions are still ordered and balanced, but the frontal symmetry gives way to deep recesses. His landscapes are no longer simply a backdrop to the action taking place in the foreground. The landscape is a part of the drama and invites entry. It becomes a part of our emotional embrace of the artwork. Titian gives us miles and miles of new "illusionistic" terrain to become emotionally involved with, and he has given himself the same terrain on which to experiment and test new-found techniques.

The towering achievements of Titian, and the course he charted for the technique of painting, are still heralded today. There is not one great painting master deserving of the name who does not owe a debt of gratitude to Titian. He elevated painting from a craft to an art, and he invested the fundamental painting techniques with transcendental significance so that those who followed him could continue to elevate that art to ever greater heights.

Vermeer and Rembrandt

During the seventeenth century, Holland was one of the world's great maritime powers. Holland had rich holdings in the East Indies and vast tracts in the Americas. Holland's preeminence is centered squarely between its successful independence from Spain in 1581, and its defeat at the hands of Charles II of England in 1664, the year New Amsterdam became New York. These years are significant for Holland in many other ways, but particularly so for painting. At no other time has the technique of painting been so successfully expanded, if success is measured by how influential these techniques remain today. The painting styles of Rembrandt and Vermeer initiated a tradition of exploring the potential of the painting medium that continues to this day.

Vermeer and Rembrandt each contributed to the technique of oil painting in a singular way. They had sharp perceptions, both sensory and emotional, of the world around them. They used what means were available to express these perceptions, and when these proved inadequate to convey how they truly felt, they went about inventing their own means.

Vermeer's approach to improving technical methods bordered on that of a scientific experiment. He used a *camera obscura* to help him discover now shapes are molded by light. He had a keen interest in optics, and was a friend of the astronomer Anton Leevanhoek (1632–1723).

Vermeer's paintings have an airy richness and depth, like a painted holograph. He achieved this polished surface through purely technical means. His paintings give direct evidence of his scientific inquisitiveness. The luster found in his works is a property of the paint that Vermeer discovered by means of patient and painstaking glazing. It was a technical advance that allowed him to express his spirit.

Vermeer was fortunate to be heir and privy to a great tradition of painting techniques that began two centuries before his birth. The early northern masters invented painting in oils. The work of the early Dutch and Flemish masters have a gemlike brilliance as if they were painted yesterday. This is evidence of a sound and enduring technique. Vermeer took advantage of this tradition and impressed upon them his own personal stamp. His glassy surface remains an enigma and will always retain its inquisitive character for future generations to marvel.

Rembrandt was an artist of rare talents who was able to excel because the prevailing style of his time had reached an impasse. It is easy to understand how the Renaissance system could have produced and nurtured a Michelangelo or a Raphael. The appearance of a Rembrandt is harder to fathom.

No other painter's life was so much an expression of achievement through technique. Anyone familiar with the body of Rembrandt's work immediately recognizes the chronology of the paintings. It represents the very evolution of pictorial effects in painting. The graphic gives way to a density counterbalanced to an evanescence.

Rembrandt's success is partly due to his northern heritage. Northerners were by nature adverse to the ideal conceptions being practiced and preached in Rome. Painting in Rome was conceived as teaching by example. The viewer was meant to enter into communion with the ideal by way of union. In the North, painting was used more with participation in mind, and the viewer was invited to join the scene by means of identification.

If one word could be found to sum up Rembrandt's approach to his art, it would be fidelity. Rembrandt creates a space that the viewer can enter. It is the epitome of the northern emphasis on participation. His figures relate to each other as if emerging from a common element. In later works, such as the *Return of the Prodigal,* the interaction almost takes on disturbing proximity. We are made keenly aware of the gravity of the situation. The paintings take on a gravity of their own, yet it is our own gravity as well, and its pull is inescapable.

Rembrandt achieves this communion with his paintings most tellingly in his self-portraits, a subject of which he has the most to reveal. Rembrandt's self-portraits speak to us and say, "Look at me, I am a man, with all the weaknesses and foibles to which a man is susceptible." We can identify with Rembrandt because his work completely lacks any sense of egocentricism. Being egocentric is a quality of being so wrapped up in oneself that a barrier is placed between a sincere communication with fellow human beings.

To say that Rembrandt was a great technician is an understatement. All of the painters of his time were well trained and displayed varying degrees of excellence. Rembrandt was not as facile with the paintbrush as was Frans Hals (1580–1666). But while Hals's brush-strokes weave a textual surface to his subject matter, Rembrandt's brush penetrates past the surface and explores the impenetrable depths of an object's weight. He makes us feel as if we are made of the same stuff. His brush could climb a ridge of paint, and with a twist of his wrist, make his line submerge almost into the intricacies of the canvas itself.

The basic rudiments of painting techniques during the baroque era had remained unchanged for one hundred years before Rembrandt's time. The basic tenets had been laid down by the proto-baroque masters, Titian, Tintoretto, and Correggio. This made for a situation ripe for exploitation. Rembrandt did so by softening the rigidity that still defined pictorial space in both the North and the South. He explored the vicissitudes of the oil medium by creating deep transparencies and flittering surfaces. He daubed with brushes and scraped with knifes, producing untold variegated textures.

Rembrandt's greatest achievements in painting were never acknowledged in his lifetime. He painted with singularity of purpose, to convince those who looked at his paintings of the intensity of his feelings toward his subject matter. His contemporaries had conditioned their own eyes to seeing in a certain manner, and were blind to Rembrandt's achievements. To say that Rembrandt was ahead of his time is the same as saying that he was able to project himself into the future, and indeed it took art scholarship one hundred and fifty years to finally recognize Rembrandt's triumphs.

Goya

The life of Francisco José Goya crosses from the neoclassical into the romantic eras. However, he cannot be characterized as belonging to either movement. Goya's mind operated on a level that would not allow him to subscribe to an ideal that left life fatuous as did these two movements. The chaos that shook Europe during the first quarter of the nineteenth century swept away any pretense of logic. Aided by his own deafness and despondency, Goya painted a brutal world of hypocrisy.

Goya can be understood as the alembic through which art changed from that of an "enlightened" society to one of an alienated society. Goya painted a world where in the end, all is madness. Kings and queens sit on throwns eating cake, and men are tortured to death for exercising choice and showing courage.

As court painter to King Charles IV of Spain, Goya remained relatively isolated from the art movement in the rest of Europe. He visited Rome only once, and never became indoctrinated in neoclassicism. He painted life honestly, not allowing his subjects to hide behind idealized conceptions. When Goya painted the royal family as contemptible, it is Goya's own contempt that inhabits the painting. It is a truly intersubjective message aimed at those who look at the painting.

Goya was well armed to make this message understood. He commanded the rare facility of technique that allowed his paintbrush to become an extension of his intuitive expressions. His brushstrokes spell emotion. Goya's paintings bare witness to his soul, from its moments of tenderness and sensuality, to those of revulsion and disgust.

Goya also used a technique known as "open color," the delineation of figures by their contours, with no addition of modeled color or light. This technique was first developed by Tintoretto (Jacopo Robusti [1518–1594]) when painting angels and other heavenly apparitions. It imparts an "other worldly" quality to the configurations. This also is the effect in the work of Goya; an introduction of another order of reality.

Goya's sentiment fits more into the romantic spirit than the classical; however, Goya is no romantic. His was a raw and expressive disillusionment. While the romantics choose sumptuous subject matter—lush, suggestive, and inviting—Goya depicted human depravity in harsh terms. The romantics were intoxicating, and invited the viewer to fancifully engage in the orgy. Goya was stupefying; he terrorized viewers to question, might this not all be a nightmarish dream?

Cezanne

The work of Paul Cezanne (1839–1906) represents the most radical departure from convention ever undertaken by an artist. Because Cezanne removed many of the rigors that a proficient technique was established to deal with, he was able to pursue his artistic investigation without being hampered by his lack of technical skills. Indeed, Cezanne scorned the academicians and referred to them as "imbeciles."

Cezanne's first step was to liberate his work from the principle of atmospheric perspective. He introduced an equalized color scheme: the colors in the background of his paintings appear with the same intensity as those in the foreground. His next step was to shatter the traditional single-point perspective with the introduction of multiple viewpoints. This allowed Cezanne to focus all of his attention on structure.

He succeeded in his artistic investigation because he held on to the single most important component of painting for an artist who is concerned with structure—namely, composition. By discarding atmospheric perspective and single-point perspective, Cezanne was able to construct paintings beyond the reach of other artists. His landscapes are constructed with the bedrock surety of a mason. His paintings are compressed under their own weight, nothing is ever left dangling. Cezanne was able to advance the technique of composition by freeing his work from limits and restrictions.

His innovations lead Cezanne directly to cubism—a reduction in space to recessional flatness, and objects are reduced to a relation of planes. Emphasis is completely removed from the specific mechanics that are required to reproduce sensory qualities: the color of a face, or the darkness of a night. This imposed strict limitations on how far cubism could be used as a means of artistic expression. There are far more ways of expressing the physiognomy of a face, or the geography of a land, than there are that of a plane. This is borne out by cubism's short reign as a vehicle for authentic expression. The major cubists from 1906 to 1920 all nurtured their own sterotypic version of the movement and then the trend died out. Those who continued to use the idiom were more in the line of commercial profiteers who contributed nothing in terms of technical advances.

Cezanne lived into the twentieth century. He witnessed the arrival of the Industrial Revolution, and he saw humans being displaced and reduced. There is no better visual example of this than Cezanne's paintings: they become more and more anonymous, with all specific characteristics becoming homogenized.

Cezanne had true artistic intelligence. There is something given in his paintings that seems primordial, down to the bare essence. He discarded the techniques of the journeymen and liberated painting from sentimental embellishment. Painting was liberated from technique, and technique was given its deathblow in the same swing.

What actually happened was that technique itself was liberated, which is a contradiction in terms. Artists were freed to use whatever means they could think of as the manner of their artistic expression. Achievement and success, which are a technique's reason for being, lost any semblance of objective validity, and were reduced to arbitrary subjectivism.

Picasso

Pablo Picasso (1881–1973) is justifiably the most important and influential artist of the twentieth century. Importance, however, does not necessarily reflect a positive influence. Picasso holds this title not by virtue of any innovative quality in his overall technique, but by freeing the artist from what were considered the constraints of technique. If Picasso did possess any towering technical abilities, they resided in his graphic skills. In his youth, Picasso showed a poetic imagination coupled with an adequate technique. However, his youthful skills dissipated as he indulged in a self-centered spontaneity of creative production.

Picasso's post-impressionist work, the paintings from the blue and pink periods that predate his moves into cubism and a pseudo-primitivism, are the best work that were produced at their time. They were the best more for want of excellence by the other post-impressionists than for any outstanding quality of their own. Technically, they were not original. Picasso relied heavily on his predecessors and borrowed from Edgar Degas (1834–1917) and Honoré Daumier (1808–1879). In point of composition they are also derivative, mostly of the expressionists. However, these paintings do express the mood of their time. There is a feeling of society being lulled into a trance. "Progress" was something very much to be endured. Picasso always remained an idealist in this sense. Throughout his entire career he presented his art as an ideal world. The conceptual, or conjecture on what art could possibly be about never enters into Picasso's work. He had very firm ideas about life and art. This is demonstrated by the quote attributed to him when asked, "What are you searching for in your art?" to which he replied, "I do not search, I find."

Picasso's cubist period marks the end of the flowering of his native skills. His cubist paintings are important visual documents; however, they rely too heavily on the raw material mined by Cezanne, the true innovator of the cubist idiom. The reduction of space to recessional flatness also introduces a perfunctory quality on the technical level into all of Picasso's efforts. This perfunctory quality was taken to an applied level in his "synthetic" period, and bordered on caricature on his sojourns to arcadia. What unites all of these early works is their strength and range of graphic abilities. Picasso gives credence to all of his anthropomorphic forms. His analytic portraits of 1908 still maintain an anatomical axiomatic certainty. His synthetic musicians resemble mechanized humanoids. This has transcendental significance. Picasso shared an expressive intuition about the human form and we as viewers participate in the communication of the idea.

Picasso's expressive abilities as a draftsman remained with him throughout his life. Yet it only asserted itself in his graphic output, namely, his drawings and his prints. Strangely, this quality is not maintained in his painting. Picasso's distortions become anatomically unwarranted. They are transgressions against our intuition. Technique becomes an object of Picasso's contempt. Brushstrokes are amassed without coherence. Distortion of the human anatomy is not exploited, it is despoiled.

If an anatomical distortion looses its axiomatic plausability, it looses its intuitive foundation. A canon of representation can be stretched to any limit before which it breaks, and therein lies an ironic twist. The stricter the canon of representation, the more obvious or exaggerated will any distortion appear. The more expressive or "personal" the manner of representation, the less radical will the distortion become. Totally amorphous configurations can assume anthropomorphic characteristics, objectified in concepts of "action," "gesture," and "process." Technique is meaningless among this personal type of art.

The artist who chooses the more difficult path, of giving expressive significance to anatomy while adhering to strict canons of representation is engaged in an activity far more singular in its achievement. Adding expressive significance to the classical ideal in anatomy would be a Herculean task. The referendum on Picasso is therefore a "split decision." His graphic skills at depicting humanity knew no limit, paralleled only by his ability to manipulate and control those around him. Picasso carefully cultivated his public images, and his audience became spellbound by the glowering clown, the minotaur in boxer shorts, and "comrade" Picasso.

CONCLUDING REMARKS

The subjective message of the artist has a multifarious nature. First, it is deep and personal, a reflection of an artist's inner feelings. But it must also be intersubjective. It must enter into communication. An artist's identity is formed by the reception of his or her art object by its audience. It also must cross the void as an objective apparition. It is across objectivity that the subjective message must be carried. Because objective existence is always "progressing," and because the subjective beings themselves are always in a process of coming into and passing out of existence, the nature of the communicative message is always in a state of change as well. Modern eyes have undergone a conditioning process not granted to those of years past. We view art work from a completely different perspective, and the artwork's meaning has developed and changed as well. This "extra-aesthetic" quality of the artwork is transcendence itself, the artist's transcendent residue forever inoculating in objectivity, forever changing, relentlessly.

This is why it is so important to admit that an artwork is nothing but an illusion. It must always retain its elusiveness. Paintings of rainbows are not rainbows. They are an illusion of a rainbow, an objective representation. The illusion is kept alive in our minds. We all see and feel differently about rainbows, from rapture to indifference. That is because we are all different. The painting of the rainbow remains elusive in its receptivity to all of our different feelings and ideas.

However, the work of art that attempts to give objective expression to a subjective feeling without making reference to objective existence has lost all of its elusiveness. The subjective message has been narrowly proscribed down to the singularity of the artist's subjectivity. Therefore the reception of the communicative message also becomes highly personal and subjective. The communication of the message is not like the meeting of long lost friends, or even the meeting of new friends. It is rather like that of two lonely ships passing in the night.

The intersubjective message transmitted during aesthetic communication must either weigh anchor or set sail for port. It cannot drift. Technique is the anchor upon which the subjective message finds objective expression and validity. It provides a map for those who participate to find their way, to know where they are going, where they have been; and, most importantly, suggests the final destination where some day we will all meet.

Bibliography

Burckhardt, Jacob. *Force and Freedom.* New York: Meridian Books, 1955.

Descartes, René. *Discourse on Method and the Meditations.* London: Penguin Books, 1968.

Jaspers, Karl. *Man in the Modern Age.* Garden City, N.Y.: Doubleday Books, 1957.

Jung, C. G. *Psyche and Symbol: A Selection from the Writings of C. G. Jung.* New York: Anchor Books, 1958.

Kant, Immanuel. *Critique of Pure Reason.* New York: St. Martins Press, 1965.

Merleau-Ponty, Maurice. *The Phenomenology of Perception.* London: Routledge & Kegan Paul, 1962.

Radin, Paul. *Primitive Religion.* New York: Dover, 1957.

Ricoeur, Paul. *Freedom and Nature.* Northwestern University Press, 1966.

Sartre, Jean-Paul. *Being and Nothingness.* New York: Washington Square Press, 1966.

Index